Getting into
Law

Emily Lucas

12th edition

trotman | t

Getting into guides

Getting into Art & Design Courses, 10th edition
Getting into Business & Economics Courses, 12th edition
Getting into Dental School, 10th edition
Getting into Engineering Courses, 4th edition
Getting into Law, 12th edition
Getting into Medical School 2019 Entry, 23rd edition
Getting into Oxford & Cambridge 2019 Entry, 21st edition
Getting into Pharmacy and Pharmacology Courses, 2nd edition
Getting into Physiotherapy Courses, 9th edition
Getting into Psychology Courses, 12th edition
Getting into Veterinary School, 11th edition
How to Complete Your UCAS Application 2019 Entry, 30th edition

Getting into Law

This 12th edition published in 2018 by Trotman Education, an imprint of Crimson Publishing Ltd, 21d Charles Street, Bath BA1 1HX.

© Crimson Publishing Ltd 2018

Author: Emily Lucas

11th edn: Steven Boyes and Melanie Allen

British Library Cataloguing in Publication Data
A catalogue record for this book is available from the British Library.

ISBN 978 1 911067 78 8

Printed and bound in Malta by Gutenberg Press Ltd

Contents

Contents

Preface

Law has always been a sought after profession for students, and now, perhaps more than ever before, aspiring lawyers face tough competition at virtually every stage of their route to qualification, from securing a place on one of the 'best' university law degree courses to finding a job at the end of it all.

During the course of MPW's work advising students on their choice of university course and subsequent career path, we have gathered together a huge amount of information on law courses and the legal profession. With the encouragement of Trotman Publishing, that information has been brought together in this guide.

This edition has been substantially revised and updated. We hope that this guide will be useful to anyone considering a career in law.

MPW
November 2017

About the author

Emily Lucas read medical science at the University of Birmingham before joining MPW Birmingham to teach biology in 2013. She currently holds the position of University Support Officer and helps students with their applications as well as supporting students with preparation for university entrance examinations.

Acknowledgements

First of all, I would like to thank MPW and Trotman Education for giving me the opportunity to produce this edition of *Getting into Law*. Many thanks are due to all those who have written previous editions.

I would like to thank all of the individuals who have contributed to the book, especially Kevin Gilbert, Sarah Hall, David Sharpe, His Honour Judge Jinder Singh Boora, Ben Tambling, Uthman Ali, Alesha Ghani, Peter Summerville, Ela Oluwole, Andrew Kirkpatrick, Stewart White, Shidul Hoque and Cameron Stewart, for their insights into applying to law courses, as well as studying and working in the field of law. In addition, I would like to thank Rebecca Jefferson, Ela Oluwole and Zara Azmat for allowing me to reproduce their personal statements here as successful examples; I am extremely grateful that these individuals were willing to take time out of their busy schedules to contribute.

I also owe an enormous debt of gratitude to Alex Moran, for her guidance and willingness to lend her political knowledge to ensure that students can find an insightful current affairs section in this book. Countless students have benefitted from her intellect and will now hopefully continue to do so.

I would like to thank those at the Law Society, the Solicitors Regulation Authority, the Bar Council of England and Wales and the Bar Standards Board, as well as the university admissions departments, law firms and barristers' chambers who have responded to my endless pestering regarding statistics and advice.

Finally, I would like to thank all of the students who I have worked with on their university applications over the last few years. Supporting students with their university applications is among my favourite aspects of my job, and much of the insight offered here was developed through these experiences.

About this book

This book is written for anyone considering a career in law. Law is a perennial favourite as a career choice: it offers intellectual stimulation, ancient customs, a morally satisfying focus on justice and fairness, and potentially great financial rewards.

However, with popularity comes competition: now, more than ever before, competition for places to read law at university, solicitors' training contract places and barristers' pupillages is intense. You will therefore need to do your research and be as fully prepared as possible. I hope that this book will go some way towards arming you with the necessary information to help you to succeed.

The book will start with an introduction to the legal profession, an overview of the UK's legal systems, and a discussion of what lawyers do and how they fit into the legal systems.

The next two chapters will then outline how to qualify as a lawyer, including the different qualification routes, and then consider the importance of work experience.

The remaining chapters will guide you through the university application process, including choosing the right university law (or other) course, completing the UCAS form (including the all-important personal statement), preparing for an interview if necessary and what to do on results day. There is then a chapter outlining the arrangements for fees and funding for university degree courses.

At the end of the book there is a glossary of terms, relating to studying law, applying to university and qualifying as a lawyer.

Of course, you will still have to show lots of ability and drive to impress university law admissions tutors and your potential future employers. You should make sure that you:

- revise thoroughly for your exams and get the best grades you possibly can, giving you the widest choice of degree options.
- become a legal eagle and do your own research. Talk to your teachers, family, friends, lawyers and anyone else who knows something about the legal profession. Consider carefully what type of degree course is appropriate for you, or, indeed, whether you should even study law and become a lawyer in the first place. There is also a huge amount of information and guidance online, which the references in this book will help you find, so make sure that you use it!

1 | An introduction to the legal profession

Most people's first impressions of the legal profession come from the glamorous world of film and television. Legal dramas paint a picture of lawyers striding heroically across the courtroom of life, standing up for truth and justice. But what are lawyers and what do they actually do?

The term 'lawyer' is a loose one that covers barristers, solicitors, judges, legal executives, paralegals, in-house legal advisors, some civil servants and academic lawyers. In England and Wales, the crucial distinction to make is between the two main branches of the profession: solicitors and barristers. The legal professions in Scotland and Northern Ireland have a similar distinction and are outlined at the end of Chapter 3. The essential difference between solicitors and barristers relates to their respective rights to advocate on behalf of a client in court: traditionally only barristers were permitted to undertake advocacy on behalf of a client in the highest courts. This distinction means that law is sometimes referred to as a 'split' profession – but in fact the split is increasingly becoming blurred, due to modern reforms that permit solicitors to undertake further training and then represent clients in the higher courts. (The term 'attorney' is American and has no real meaning in the UK.)

Solicitors work on all aspects of the law, but do not normally present their clients' cases in court.

Barristers are instructed by solicitors to represent their clients in the courtroom or give opinions on specific points of law.

The main focus of this book is on the solicitors' and barristers' professions, but there are many other careers within the legal field that can also be pursued, and also many non-legal careers for which a law degree might provide a good foundation. More information on this is given in the paragraphs below.

Solicitors

Solicitors are often described as being like medical general practitioners (GPs). They deal directly with their clients and often have an ongoing professional and/or business relationship with them. Solicitors in private practices group together in law firm partnerships, with the senior solicitors being partners and the more junior solicitors being employed assistants. Most solicitors now deal with specific areas of the law, for example employment or family law or, in the City, specialist areas such as syndicated loans, bonds or takeovers and mergers. In this respect they differ from GPs, who are usually generalists.

However, in most cases, law firms cover a wide area of legal practice; this means that in smaller firms solicitors may be required to cover a broader range of areas, whereas the larger law firms will have specialists in very narrow areas of law.

Historically, solicitors could only appear in lower courts, such as the magistrates' and county courts. These days, however, solicitors who obtain higher rights of audience can appear in the higher courts, including the Supreme Court, and may even apply to become QCs (Queen's Counsel), although this is still rare.

The Law Society is the body that represents and supports solicitors in England and Wales. The Solicitors Regulation Authority is the independent regulator of solicitors and law firms in England and Wales, and deals with all regulatory and disciplinary matters, including:

- setting the standards for qualifying as a solicitor
- administering the roll (register) of solicitors
- drafting the rules of professional conduct
- monitoring solicitors and their firms to make sure that they are complying with the rules.

Barristers

Barristers have traditionally been described as more like medical consultants. They are 'self-employed referral professionals' who are often, although not exclusively, trial lawyers – meaning that they appear robed and wigged in court on behalf of their clients. Clients are usually referred to them by a professional advisor, often a solicitor – although modern reforms allow barristers to see the public directly where the Bar Council has agreed that no referral is necessary (for example in relation to tax advice when referred by an accountant).

It is usual for barristers (often called counsel) to specialise in certain areas of law, such as criminal law, company law or tax law and so on. Barristers in private practice group together in chambers, sharing overheads and office support, but remaining self-employed professionals.

Barristers in England and Wales are represented by the Bar Council, which promotes barristers' services and upholds ethical standards in the profession. The Bar Standards Board performs a similar function to the Solicitors Regulation Authority, and is responsible for regulating barristers in the public interest. Its functions include:

- setting the education and training requirements for becoming a barrister
- setting the standards of conduct for barristers
- monitoring the service provided by barristers.

Legal executives

Legal executives are lawyers who have not undertaken the professional training required to become a solicitor or barrister, but have qualified instead with the Chartered Institute of Legal Executives (CILEx). Historically, the modern legal executive role evolved from the role of law clerks, who used to help solicitors with their cases. In the 1960s, the legal executives' profession was created in order to offer a recognised career path.

The Legal Services Act 2007 made chartered legal executives 'authorised persons' who are able to undertake 'reserved legal activities' alongside solicitors and barristers. Qualified chartered legal executives can now do much of the same work that solicitors do, but are trained to work in one or two areas of the law rather than having a broader, more general, legal training like solicitors. They can become partners in law firms and even judges.

Legal executives are regulated by CILEx, which offers various routes into qualifying as a legal executive. It is possible to become a qualified legal executive without having obtained a degree, and training comprises two stages. The first stage requires the completion of the CILEx Level 3 Professional Diploma in Law and Practice, which is an academic training course that provides its students with a thorough grounding in all areas of law. This is followed by the CILEx Level 6 Professional Diploma in Higher Law and Practice. In addition, those following this route are expected to complete three years of qualifying employment.

There is also a graduate fast-track diploma for those who have obtained a law degree or Graduate Diploma in Law (see 'Do I need a law degree?' below). The Institute offers an accessible and cost-effective route to becoming a lawyer. Completion typically takes nine months to one year, and can be studied either on a distance-learning basis or at a qualifying centre. Further information is available at www.cilex.org.uk.

Other lawyers

The Legal Services Act 2007 also defined various other groups of lawyers as being entitled to undertake reserved legal activities. These lawyers are trained and qualified in particular specialist areas of law and often work in law firms alongside solicitors. They are notaries, licensed conveyancers, law costs draftsmen, trademark agents and patent agents. Further information can be found at www.thenotariessociety.org.uk (for notaries), www.clc-uk.org (for licensed conveyancers), www.associationofcostslawyers.co.uk (for law costs draftsmen), www.itma.org.uk (trademark agents) and www.cipa.org.uk (for patent agents).

Case study

Kevin is a Licensed Conveyancer whose route into law followed more of a non-traditional route. After completing his GCSEs, he secured a job as a junior clerk at a leading barristers' chambers.

'This was my introduction into the world of law and it provided me with a brilliant overview of many areas of law and how the legal system worked, including who was responsible for what and, more importantly, how fascinating the work was.

'I soon realised that being a clerk was not for me; it was the jobs of the solicitors and legal executives that I found particularly interesting. As a result, I opted to study an introductory law course (which is now part of the CILEx route). During this time, I managed to secure a job at a solicitors' firm as an assistant, allowing me to gain a fascinating insight into law and gain valuable on-the-job experience while continuing my studies. At the end of my course, I received a promotion into the Land and Property team. The firm offered to pay for my further education via the CILEx route, which comprised undertaking two courses (which provided an in-depth knowledge of all areas of law before specialising) over a period of four years. This involved going to the local university twice a week during the evening.

'During the term of this course, I continued to work in the Land and Property team and found that I had a very unusual fondness for land and property and the law surrounding it, thanks to the extremely enthusiastic solicitor with whom I worked. I was probably the only person on my course that actually flourished during the land law section, with the rest of the class being more interested in the more exciting areas such as criminal law!

'After some time, I moved firms and I was asked whether I would consider crossing over to the role of a Licensed Conveyancer,

---

which is a much more specialist area solely concentrating on the areas of land law, contract law and conveyancing itself. Given this was my area of interest and the area in which I had acquired the most experience, I relished the opportunity to take this on. I had some exemptions from the CLC (Council for Licensed Conveyancers) course, but it still involved fitting further study via distance learning in around a full-time job; and, as I was given more responsibility, I found it challenging to prioritise my assignments. During this time, I changed job three times, allowing me to gain further experience in different areas of property law. By building up a broader range of experience and knowledge across a variety of fields, I had more to offer clients and potential employers.

'After finishing the CLC course, I completed a period of qualifying employment – almost like a training contract – before I was granted a practising certificate. This involved me completing a checklist of various matters and issues confirming that I was competent in my field and able to demonstrate that I had the knowledge and capabilities to work on my own without supervision. It took around eight years to qualify, but I found that the experience I gained while studying was invaluable to my progression and employability. Once qualified, I began working at a new firm and was appointed director within ten months. In this position, I oversee the work of two solicitors and about eight support staff. I am responsible for compliance, money laundering, business development and, ulti-mately, the proper running and management of the practice to ensure it continues to thrive and grow.'

Size and make-up of the legal profession (England and Wales)

Solicitors

The solicitors' profession in England and Wales is the largest branch of the legal profession. In October 2017, the Law Society (www.lawsociety.org.uk), which acts as the governing body for solicitors, reported that there were 184,736 registered solicitors, and 142,515 of these held a practising certificate. To qualify as a solicitor, you would normally be expected to complete a training contract period of employment that lasts two years. In October 2017, the Law Society reported that there were 5,733 trainee registrations.

The solicitors' profession is divided between solicitors who work in private practice for law firms and those who work 'in-house' (i.e. for companies, government legal departments and so on). In 2016, there were 10,430 private law firms employing 91,116 solicitors, meaning that 67% of all practising solicitors were working in private practice. The number of solicitors employed outside private practice amounted to 26,894. In 2016, almost 40.4% of practising solicitors were located in London, with just over 25% working in City firms.

Of all the practising solicitors in 2017, 88,010 were women, meaning that women now account for 50.2% of all solicitors on roll. Around 62% of new registrations were women. The proportion of practising solicitors who are from minority ethnic groups continues to grow and was 16% in 2017.

Barristers

The barristers' profession, known as the Bar, is much smaller than the solicitors' profession. According to the Bar Standards Board (www.barstandardsboard.org.uk), there were a total of 16,435 barristers in practice in December 2017, of whom 37% were women and 13% described themselves as belonging to an ethnic minority. Most practising barristers (13,076 in 2017) are self-employed. A further 2,970 barristers are in employed practice.

	Number	% women (approx)	% in London (approx)
Solicitors	136,176	49%	40.4%
– private practice	– 91,116		
– in-house	– 26,894		
Barristers	16,435	37%	61.5%
– self-employed	– 13,076		
– employed	– 2,970		

Table 1: Solicitors and barristers in practice (England and Wales), most recent statistics available

Legal executives and other lawyers

The much younger legal executives' profession is smaller still: the Chartered Institute of Legal Executives (www.cilex.org.uk) reported in 2015 that there were around 7,500 qualified chartered legal executives, of whom 250 were partners in law firms. The total number of members of the Institute (including paralegals and other legal professionals) was around 20,000, of whom 74% were women. More than a third of their new members are of an ethnic minority.

The other groups of lawyers mentioned above (notaries, licensed conveyancers, law costs draftsmen, trademark agents and patent agents) are also much smaller in number than solicitors or barristers. This book will therefore focus on the two main branches of the legal profession: solicitors and barristers.

Gender balance

It is difficult to imagine that less than 100 years ago the legal profession was the preserve of men. Things have changed and are still changing. The Law Society reports that just over 60% of training contracts are now issued to women. About 49% of practising solicitors are female, and, in July 2016, there were nearly 8,105 women partners in law firms. Around 60% of practising solicitors under the age of 35 are now women. The Law Society's most recent report suggests that the number of women practising as solicitors is almost equal to the number of men in 2017. There has been a feeling within the solicitors' profession in the past that not enough female solicitors make it to partnership in some of the very large law firms, and there is still a substantial difference between the representation of men and women at partner level, with women currently representing 33% of partners. In larger firms with more than 50 partners, there is an even smaller percentage of female partners: 27%, with a 35% representation in smaller firms (typically two to five partners). However, the gap has been narrowing over recent years. The percentage of women solicitors working outside private practice, i.e. in-house, is higher.

About 36% of practising barristers are women, with 51% of new entrants undertaking pupillage being female. Whereas in the past it was difficult for women to break down the traditional barriers, today the profession is increasingly open to all. This is evident in the fact that in 2016–17 just under 53% of barristers called to the Bar were women.

However, there is still progress to be made by women in terms of judicial appointments. Only 28% of all judges in England and Wales are women, only nine out of 37 Appeal Court judges are women, and only two women have made it to the most senior judicial appointment (a Supreme Court judge). Efforts are being made to increase the number of female judges and the number is increasing every year. It will, however, take time before parity can be reached.

The majority (74%) of members of the Chartered Institute of Legal Executives are women.

Chapter 3 contains more details about the legal profession, where lawyers work, and what they do. Chapter 4 contains details about how to qualify as a lawyer.

Do I need a law degree?

The legal profession in England and Wales is virtually unique in not requiring all entrants to have a law degree. In fact, many non-law graduates enter the profession through the full-time Graduate Diploma in Law programme, which is an intensive one-year postgraduate course for non-law graduates covering the essential foundation subjects taught as part of a law degree. A substantial percentage of non-law graduates are direct entrants into the solicitors' profession. Similarly, around 46% of UK-domiciled students enrolled on the Bar Professional Training Course (BPTC) in cohorts from 2011–12 to 2015–16 had a non-law related undergraduate background. This clearly demonstrates that the skills acquired on many non-law degrees are often highly sought after by legal recruiters. For example, language skills or scientific/technical skills may be particularly useful in certain areas of law, and humanities degrees teach and test many of the skills that are essential for a lawyer, such as the ability to research information and analyse and present it in a clear and concise way. It is therefore important to bear in mind that you do not need a law degree to become a lawyer and many employers positively welcome applications from non-law graduates who can offer broader skills in other areas. There are, however, cost implications due to the extra year of postgraduate study that will be required (see Chapter 4, page 47 for more details).

It is also important to be aware that not every law degree is recognised by the professional bodies as a qualifying law degree (QLD) that will satisfy the requirements for the academic stage of training. It depends on the subjects that are studied on the course. This means that, if you do decide to do a law degree, you must be careful when choosing your course. The Solicitors Regulation Authority (SRA) and the Bar Standards Board (BSB) keep registers of which degrees are approved QLDs and these are available on their respective websites. See Chapter 6 for further details.

Similarly, many students graduate with degrees in law and then, for whatever reason, do not go on to qualify as a solicitor or barrister. The number of law graduates compared with the number of professional training places available is very telling: according to the most recent figures from the Law Society, in 2016, 15,950 students graduated with law degrees from universities in England and Wales, which was 3.4% higher than in 2015. This number continues to rise each year: it was 12,858 in 2006 and 14,859 in 2009. The number of law graduates in England and Wales in 2016 was therefore 24% higher than in 2006. These figures only include those with 'straight' law degrees and not those with joint honours degrees that include law, so the total number of law graduates is likely to be considerably higher.

However, the limited number of training places available means that many undergraduate law students do not carry on to qualify as solicitors or barristers. The number of solicitors' training contracts registered annually has, according to the Law Society, remained stable at around 5,000 since 2009–10. In the legal year 2015–16, only 424 aspiring barristers obtained their first six months' pupillage, which is the first part of the mandatory 12-month training stage for those who want to prac-tise as a barrister. Some law graduates will also enter the legal profession via the graduate fast-track diploma to become legal executives, but there are still considerably more law graduates than entrants to the legal professions. Therefore, the link between taking a law degree and becoming a qualified lawyer is not nearly as clear-cut as many people believe, and one definitely does not imply the other.

What if I don't want to go into the law after my degree?

As well as those who, unfortunately, do not manage to get into one of the legal professions after taking a law degree, there are also some students who study law with no intention of becoming a professional lawyer. The legal knowledge and additional skills gained from a law degree are highly prized and can be applied to a number of jobs.

But what else can a law graduate do other than law? Many public figures have degrees in law that have led them in all sorts of different directions, from politicians to comedians. Some of the careers that a law degree can lead to are listed below.

- **Accountancy.** Many aspects of accountancy relate to those found in legal practice, such as analysing large amounts of technical material, writing reports and advising clients. Law graduates are often particularly attracted by tax consultancy.
- **Civil service.** If you are interested in policy making and implementation, then you might think about a career in the civil service. Administrators such as civil servants need a methodical and precise approach, as well as good writing and communication skills – all skills that are developed and honed on a law degree course. Some government departments, such as the Home Office, HM Revenue & Customs, the Ministry of Justice and the Foreign & Commonwealth Office, have particular legal responsibilities and might be especially attractive to law graduates. Local government and the health services are also possibilities for public sector careers in administration.
- **Commerce and industry.** The skills you learn from a law degree will also be invaluable in the world of commerce and industry, where there are career opportunities in general business management.
- **Banking and finance.** A number of law graduates are lured into the highly paid world of banking and finance, where a legal background can certainly be useful.

Law graduates also go into many other areas, such as legal publishing, the media, journalism (legal or otherwise), the police service, teaching, human resources and more.

Some law graduates choose not to pursue the training to become either a solicitor or a barrister, or, indeed a legal executive, but would still like to do something in the legal field. They will often move into areas such as paralegal or clerking work. Paralegals research cases, scan and collate documents and generally assist qualified lawyers in their work. Clerks undertake duties such as taking witness statements on behalf of solicitors' clients and conducting legal research for solicitors, barristers and others plus any administrative work that is required.

Case study

Sarah completed her undergraduate degree in law at the University of Birmingham in 2017, and secured a prestigious graduate role as a tax associate at one of the Big Four.

'I was always torn between following my passion for performing arts and law. Having initially decided to attend performing arts college, I realised that I missed the challenge of academia and decided to change my plans and attend a sixth-form college so that I could study A levels and apply for law as an undergraduate degree.

'Despite performing well in my degree, I struggled to land a legal training contract. Thankfully, I had considered alternative careers and successfully acquired a graduate role as a tax associate for one of the Big Four. I now work in international tax services (ITS) and although this sounds nothing like a career in law, it is actually quite similar! I deal with legislation on a daily basis, across borders and internationally. My degree prepared me well for a commercial career: 'commercial awareness' was a bit of a buzzword at university, but it wasn't until I started my role as a tax associate that I really began to grasp what it was.

'Studying law provides you with a strong skill set overall through the rigours of such an academic subject, as well as the continuous need to develop knowledge in industry sectors and instilling a desire to succeed. The application process itself was tough and lasted around seven months in total. My background in law was a huge benefit, though – the content I was studying at university was hugely relevant, and the environment motivated me to research firms and try and keep on top of the market! Another key aspect that I believe allowed me to secure the position was the number of extra-curricular activities that I was involved in, such as pro bono work and supporting the running of committees.

'Though not obtaining a training contract was a daunting prospect, it wasn't the end of the world. In fact, it opened up masses of opportunities for me as a graduate, and the process of applying for roles as a tax associate allowed me to identify my strengths and ensure that I stood out from other candidates.'

2| The UK's legal systems

This chapter looks predominantly at the English legal system, with the Scottish and Northern Irish legal systems briefly outlined at the end of the chapter. Welsh law mainly follows that of England, but there are a few important differences, such as the Welsh Language Act 1993, which puts the Welsh language on an equal footing with English in the conduct of public business and the administration of justice in Wales. See www.assemblywales.org for more information.

The English legal system

English law comes from two main sources: statute law made by Parliament (also known as 'Acts of Parliament' or 'legislation') and case law made by judges (also known as 'common law'). The UK's membership of the European Union and the Human Rights Act 1998 have also significantly impacted on the English legal system. These sources will be summarised below, together with a brief description of the court structure.

Statute law

Parliament is the supreme law-making body in the English legal system, and is made up of the House of Commons, the House of Lords, and the Monarch. The House of Commons is made up of 650 democratically elected Members of Parliament (MPs) from various political parties, and it is the political party that has the majority of MPs elected to the House of Commons that will form a government. It is worth noting that in 2017, there was a two-thirds vote for a snap election. Despite winning a majority in 2015, the Conservative Party failed to do so in 2017, so entered into an informal coalition with the Democratic Unionist Party (DUP), whereby the DUP aims to support governmental bills and display confidence in the government.

The House of Lords is made up of the most senior bishops in the Church of England and life peers who are nominated by the Prime Minister and then appointed by the Monarch. There are also currently 92 hereditary peers (people who have inherited their seats in the Lords) – these are eventually being phased out due to concerns about their appointment being unmeritocratic. Since the 1990s, there have been calls for reform of the House of Lords, including the suggestion that a proportion of the members be democratically elected. In May 2011, the government published detailed proposals for reform of the House of Lords, but the plans were dropped in August 2012. Instead, the House of Lords Reform Act 2014 introduced much more minor reforms, including allowing Lords to retire or be disqualified for non-attendance. Recently, Andrew Lloyd Webber retired from the House of Lords, which is something he would have been unable to do prior to these reforms. Despite these changes, the Lords as a body is often criticised, largely due to the fact that the individuals are unelected and to the phenomenon of silent peers: an estimated 300 Lords have never spoken in a debate since their appointment.

A report published in October 2017 by the speaker of the Lords, Norman Fowler, stated that in order to maintain confidence in the Chamber, it should be reduced in size to no more than 600 members, with new peers being limited to 15-year terms. At interview, you might be asked to comment on reforms such as these. See Chapter 8 for further considerations for interview preparations.

New laws are mostly put forward by the government (these are known as public bills; bills proposed by opposing parties are known as private member bills), and the draft legislation has to go through several stages of debates and votes in both the House of Commons and the House of Lords prior to its passage. In the vast majority of cases, the draft legislation has to be approved by both Houses in order for it to become law. On occasion, bills are passed back and forth between the Houses in a process known as 'parliamentary ping pong' – the Investigatory Powers Act (2016) went back and forth four times prior to its passage. The final stage in the legislative process is Royal Assent, which is where the Monarch gives approval to the draft legislation and at this point it becomes an Act of Parliament. This is merely a formality and the last time that a monarch refused assent was in 1707.

Typically, Acts of Parliament cannot be challenged by the courts, and can only be changed by a subsequent piece of legislation. Acts of Parliament are also known as 'primary legislation' because they are made by Parliament, the supreme law-making body. Parliament can delegate its law-making power to other bodies, including government departments and local authorities, and law made by such bodies is known as delegated legislation or secondary legislation. Delegated legislation is subject to the control of Parliament and can be challenged in the courts.

Common law

Although Parliament is the supreme law-making body, and judges are simply supposed to apply the laws made by Parliament in cases, the doctrine of judicial precedent and the rules of statutory interpretation mean that in practice judges also make law through decided cases. This is known as 'case law' or 'common law' and is a major source of law in the English legal system.

The doctrine of judicial precedent is based on the Latin maxim 'stare decisis' which means 'stand by what has been decided', so, very simply, when a judge makes a decision in a case, this should be followed in future cases that are similar. The system of precedent operates through the court hierarchy, so that only certain (higher) courts create binding precedents (precedents that must be followed in future cases). Precedents are created when a new situation or point of law comes up in a case that is not provided for in legislation and has not been decided in a previous case, so the judge has to decide the case by looking at situations that are similar and use reasoning by analogy.

When judges are applying legislation to cases before them, it is not always possible to simply take the words of the statute and decide the case, because words can have more than one meaning. In addition, new technology and changes in society can mean that it is not clear whether the legislation applies in some cases. This is where the rules of statutory interpretation come in. Some judges take a 'literal approach' of applying the ordinary meaning of the words in the legislation even if this leads to an absurd result, whereas other judges take a 'purposive approach' and decide the case based on what they think Parliament wanted to achieve through the legislation. When a judge makes an interpretation in a case, this can create a precedent so that future cases must follow this interpretation.

Cases to consider

In the USA, the Supreme Court (comprised of the nine most senior judges and appointed by the President) uses the Constitution to determine the outcomes of cases. There are two strands of judicial outlook – strict constructionist (originalist) and loose constructionist (right to privacy).

In its ruling, Roe v. Wade (1973) led to the legalisation of nationwide abortion in the United States and is viewed as seminal ruling. It has since been used to keep abortion legal, despite the plethora of pro-life groups and pro-life politicians in existence in the United States. However, this case also raises questions surrounding the Supreme Court's power – some believe that this ruling involved the judges going beyond their jurisdiction and that the US Supreme Court justices should simply guard the constitution.

Other cases related to reproductive rights that you might choose to read include:

- Planned Parenthood v. Casey

- Gonzales v. Carhart.

Common law as a source of law only works because of the system of law reporting in England and Wales; an accurate record of decided cases is kept so that it can be referred to by judges and lawyers in future cases. It is mostly decisions of the higher courts in the English legal system that are reported, and all High Court, Court of Appeal and Supreme Court cases are now available on the internet, for example from the British and Irish Legal Information Institute (www.bailii.org).

European Union law

In 1973, the UK joined the European Economic Community (EEC), which was established in 1957 by Germany, France, Italy, Belgium, the Netherlands and Luxembourg. In 1993, the EEC became the European Union (EU). Over the years European law has had an increasing impact on the legal systems of Member States. There are now 28 Member States.

The European Union produces its own primary and secondary legislation, and has its own court, the European Court of Justice. Case law has confirmed that European law is supreme over the national laws of Member States, and that national law must be interpreted in accordance with European law.

Cases to consider

In the R (Factortame Ltd) v, Secretary of State for Transport (1989) case, a group of Spanish fishermen claimed that the United Kingdom was in breach of European Union law regarding fishing boat ownership. This was the first time that the European Court of Justice restrained and overturned an Act of Parliament for contradicting European law.

On 23 June 2016, the UK voted to leave the European Union. Once the final Brexit deal has been negotiated, the UK will no longer need to adhere to European law. However, the Great Repeal Bill proposes that many European laws will simply be amalgamated into our own legal system. As such, many of the laws of the land following the country's exit from the European Union will remain unchanged.

What Brexit could mean, however, is that individuals will no longer be able to hold the UK to account for actions that are deemed contrary to the European Convention of Human Rights. For instance, in a case entitled Hurst v. United Kingdom in 2005, the UK was called to account under the convention for not allowing prisoners the right to vote. The European Court of Human Rights ruled this a breach of the convention of human rights. Once we have formally exited the European Union, depending on the kind of Brexit that is ultimately negotiated, these cases may not be escalated to an EU level, as we shall no longer be required to conform to the convention.

Human Rights Act 1998

The Human Rights Act 1998 officially incorporated the European Convention on Human Rights into the English legal system. The Convention sets out certain fundamental rights of the citizens of Europe, including the right to life, the right to a fair trial and the right to respect for private and family life. Prior to the Human Rights Act 1998, English citizens who believed that their human rights had been infringed had to take their case to the European Court of Human Rights in Strasbourg. The Human Rights Act 1998 means that such cases can now be dealt with in the courts of the English legal system.

The Human Rights Act 1998 has affected the English legal system in several other ways, including obligations that our courts must take into account any decision of the European Court of Human Rights, and, so far as is possible to do so, interpret national legislation so that it is compatible with the European Convention on Human Rights. All draft legislation must also state whether or not it is compatible with the Convention. This is intended to encourage the government and civil service to consider the human rights implications of proposed legislation before it is introduced.

In 2015, the Conservative Government proposed replacing the Human Rights Act with a British Bill of Rights. The Human Rights Act has been deemed by some as controversial, as it has been used as a means to protect individuals such as the Muslim cleric Abu Qatada, who was accused of having links to terrorist organisations, from extradition. Such discussions are important when considering the vote for the UK to leave the European Union. It is unclear, however, which rights would be protected within this proposed bill and thus how it would change the legal landscape.

Cases to consider

The Othman (Abu Qatada) v. United Kingdom (2012) case is an interesting case to consider in the context of human rights. Abu Qatada, a Jordanian national, required refugee status in the United Kingdom. Having been convicted on the grounds of terrorism, the United Kingdom planned to deport Qatada. Under Article 6 of the European Convention on Human Rights, the European Court of Human Rights ruled that Qatada could not be lawfully deported owing to the risk of torture upon his return.

Qatada was ultimately deported to Jordan on the basis that he would be tried fairly by the Jordanian State Security Court and would not be subject to torture, but the case made for considerable debate.

Other interesting cases to consider regarding the controversial elements of human rights include those associated with:

- the killers of James Bulger (1993)
- the Libyan soldiers convicted of sex attacks in the UK (2015).

Court structure

The court structure in England is divided into two systems: those courts with civil jurisdiction and those with criminal jurisdiction. Civil cases are private disputes between individuals or companies. There are many different types of civil law, including family law, employment law, the law of contract, the law of tort and commercial law. Criminal cases are where the state prosecutes people for breaking laws, even though there is usually a victim.

Most civil cases are heard, in the first instance, by the county courts, but in cases where large amounts of money are in dispute, they will initially be heard in the High Court. Appeals from both the county courts and the High Court can be made up through the court hierarchy.

All minor criminal matters are dealt with by the magistrates' court. Serious cases are referred to the crown court. Here, the case will be decided upon by a lay jury, a fundamental part of the criminal justice system. Cases can be appealed from the magistrates' court to the crown court and from there to the Court of Appeal (Criminal Division).

The highest court in the land is now the UK Supreme Court, which is the final court of appeal for civil cases throughout the UK, and for criminal cases from England, Wales and Northern Ireland. The Supreme Court replaced the Appellate Committee of the House of Lords in 2009. It only considers appeals that concern points of law of general public or constitutional importance. Each case is normally heard by five Justices of the Supreme Court. When a court is considering a point of European law it may refer to the European Court of Justice in Luxembourg for interpretation. It is worth noting that the UK Government intends to end ties with the European Court of Justice on the completion of the Brexit process. Some argue that this will allow the location of sovereignty to be returned to the UK, meaning that we have the upmost power regarding judicial decisions and that European Court of Justice rulings will have no bearing on us.

The Judicial Committee of the Privy Council is the court of final appeal for many current and former Commonwealth countries, UK overseas territories and Crown dependencies. In the year ending 31 March 2016, the Privy Council heard 43 appeals. By far the most contentious work relates to appeals against the death penalty.

Judges

In contrast with many other European countries, the judiciary in England and Wales is not a separate career. Judges are appointed from both main branches of the legal profession. Chartered legal executives can also now become judges.

Judges in the Supreme Court are known as Justices of the Supreme Court (formerly Law Lords in the House of Lords) and judges in the Court of Appeal are known as Lord or Lady Justices of Appeal. In the High Court, there are High Court judges and also masters and registrars, who hear certain types of applications.

Circuit judges, recorders and district judges are the remaining three types of judges. Circuit judges sit either in the crown court (to try criminal cases) or in the county courts (to hear civil cases). Recorders are part-time circuit judges, and district judges sit in the magistrates' courts and county courts.

Alternatively, a panel of lay magistrates can try criminal cases in the magistrates' court. They are not legally qualified or paid but are respected members of the community who sit as magistrates on a part-time basis.

New members of the judiciary are selected by the Judicial Appointments Commission, an independent body that was created specifically for this purpose following the Constitutional Reform Act 2005. The aim was to provide a fair and transparent selection process. Once appointed, judges are completely independent of both the legislature and the executive, and so are free to administer justice without fear of political interference. Justices of the Supreme Court are not selected by the Judicial Appointments Commission, but are instead selected by a special Supreme Court Selection Commission.

Case study

His Honour Judge Jinder Singh Boora is a circuit judge who, somewhat unusually, works in three different courts – Leicester, Northampton and Stoke-on-Trent – on primarily weighty criminal cases.

'As a circuit judge, I sit in on serious criminal cases such as terrorism, robbery, fraud and rape. I also undertake money claims involving private individuals and companies. Working in three different courts allows me to undertake a rich variety of work and meet many different people.

'My typical day involves conducting trials, in which people give evidence and juries decide whether an accused person is guilty. If an accused is found guilty or pleads guilty, I will sentence them. This is not necessarily imprisonment; I have other powers: for example, to direct a person to undertake work in the community, attend a drug rehabilitation course or pay a fine. The longest prison sentence I have passed so far is 20 years.

'Being a judge is different from most other professions because it can only be a second career. A judge first qualifies as a solicitor or barrister. Then, if they are successful in their career as a lawyer, they can apply to become a judge. This is usually after about 20 years in practice.

'My first career was as a barrister. I entered this profession because I had watched so many films and TV programmes about the drama of courtrooms and famous trial advocates. I was spellbound by the romantic notion of a brilliant advocate securing the acquittal of an innocent person wrongly accused.

'I did a law degree at university. While there, I undertook work experience in a solicitors' office and in barristers' chambers. This work gave me invaluable experience and fortified my view that I was destined for the bar.

'After university, I undertook the bar vocational course, which is the barristers' professional course. After that, I did pupillage, which is practical training through shadowing an experienced barrister.

'After 15 years as a barrister, I decided to apply to become a part-time judge. I was successful, and for 12 years I practised as a barrister, with occasional part-time sittings as a judge.

'Becoming a judge is a highly competitive process. The part-time judicial sittings helped lift my profile and eventually, after a number of unsuccessful applications, I became a full-time judge. Success in the interview to become a circuit judge really came from being confident in my capabilities, which involved careful reflection on my successes in the courtroom as a barrister.

'Aspiring judges should work closely with a senior lawyer or another judge on their application form. They will need to use a lot of examples to demonstrate the appropriate skills, and it is useful to find someone more senior to help you identify your strongest examples.

'Throughout your career – through work experience at under-graduate level to work as a lawyer – you should note down each time you have successfully achieved something on the job, such as communicating effectively with someone from a disadvantaged background. By doing so, preparation interviews will be much easier!'

Tribunals

A system of tribunals operates alongside the court system. Each type of tribunal specialises in a particular area of law. For example, Employment Tribunals handle workplace disputes between employers and employees. These include disputed deductions from wages, unfair dismissal, redundancy and discrimination. A tribunal is a more informal setting than a court. There are no judges; tribunals are chaired by a legally qualified tribunal judge, who will often sit with specialist non-legal members who have particular experience in the subject matter of the tribunal. In Employment Tribunals, for example, a chairman will be assisted by two lay members. There is no standard form of procedure. Nonetheless, they operate in a similar way to court proceedings, with witnesses usually giving evidence on oath.

Reform

The English legal system is constantly changing, so it is very important you keep up to date with current affairs in the legal field if you are think-ing about a legal career. Essential preparation for a legal career includes reading a good quality (i.e. broadsheet) newspaper such as *The Times*. You can also look at professional journals such as *The Law Society Gazette* and *The Lawyer*, which are both available online. Further details and website addresses are contained in Chapter 12.

The Scottish legal system

Scotland has its own legal system, with significant differences from those of the other constituent nations of the United Kingdom. The two fundamental differences are the role of the Scottish Parliament in formulating legislation, and the basis of Scottish jurisprudence in a mixed system of uncodified civil law and common law.

Since 1999, the Scottish Parliament has been responsible for legislating on a wide range of domestic matters relating to Scotland, but there are certain policy areas reserved for the UK Parliament at Westminster. Notably, these include constitutional matters, defence and national security policy, foreign policy, and fiscal and economic policy. Scotland's legal system and court structure is separate and autonomous from that of England and Wales and Northern Ireland. Historically, it has its basis in Roman law, with some English common law influence since the Act of Union of 1707. Recent developments in Scottish law have seen the strong influence of English (and other jurisdictions') common law, as well as the influence and incorporation of European Union law.

While some areas of law are similar to that of England, Scotland has its own system of criminal law and procedure, of civil procedure, and of certain areas of private law (such as land law). The court system reflects these differences, with its own system of separate criminal and civil courts. By way of illustration, the Court of Session is Scotland's supreme court for civil cases and the High Court of Justiciary is Scotland's supreme court for criminal cases. Decisions of the High Court of Justiciary are not generally subject to review by the UK Supreme Court, which reflects Scotland's distinctive tradition of criminal law and procedure. Most cases in Scotland are dealt with in either the Sheriff Court, which deals with the majority of civil cases and more serious criminal offences, or the Justice of the Peace Court, which deals with less serious criminal offences. Tribunals also sit in Scotland. The legal profession in Scotland is outlined in Chapter 3.

For more information see:
www.scotcourts.gov.uk/about-the-scottish-court-service.

The Northern Irish legal system

Like Scotland, Northern Ireland (NI) has a legal system separate from that of England and Wales. Unlike Scotland, NI's legal system to a large extent mirrors that of England and Wales, with the following differences.

In terms of legislative law, the Northern Ireland Assembly (which gained legislative powers in 1999 following the Good Friday Agreement) has the power to make laws for NI on all transferred matters, which are generally in the economic and social field. The Westminster Parliament retains responsibility for matters of national importance, such as the constitution, national security, defence and foreign policy. The Assembly operates under a unique power-sharing arrangement between the two main political communities in Northern Ireland.

NI has its own judicial system (the Northern Ireland Courts and Tribunals Service), which parallels that of England and Wales. It includes the Court of Appeal, the High Court of Justice in Northern Ireland, the crown court, magistrates' courts and county courts. The highest court of appeal for both criminal and civil matters, as in England and Wales, is the UK Supreme Court. Judicial law in NI partially derives from English common law and is based on the doctrine of judicial precedent. It has developed along very similar lines to that of English common law. English precedent from the higher courts is not, however, binding, but is deemed to be persuasive. The higher Northern Irish courts also pay attention to important decisions made in the Republic of Ireland (ROI), the major Commonwealth nations and even the USA. The legal profession in Northern Ireland will be outlined in Chapter 3.

For more information please see www.niassembly.gov.uk, www.gov.uk/guidance/devolution-settlement-northern-ireland and www.nidirect.gov.uk/index/information-and-services/crime-justice-and-law.

3 | What do lawyers do?

The legal profession in England and Wales is divided into two main branches: solicitors and barristers, as explained in Chapter 1. This chapter will run through the working practices of each of the branches of the profession in more detail. At the end of the chapter there is an overview of the legal profession in Scotland and Northern Ireland.

Solicitors

Solicitors' work is as diverse as life itself – they will be behind the scenes offering legal advice to their clients on everything from corporate takeovers to individual personal injury claims. The day-to-day tasks of a solicitor vary enormously depending on where they work. As mentioned in Chapter 1, about 67% of all practising solicitors work in private practice for law firms: the rest work in-house either for companies or for government agencies, etc. Even for those working in law firms, the work will be completely different depending on the type of firm. For example, in a large firm it is not unusual to be working as part of a team of lawyers on one large case for several months, whereas in a small firm you may have 20 or more cases on the go at one time and be solely responsible for dealing with these.

This section offers a brief overview of the different types of law firms and the sort of work that the solicitors who work in them undertake.

Large corporate firms

The largest law firms by turnover tend to be the big corporate law firms specialising in corporate and finance law, which usually have their headquarters in the City of London. Most of them also have large international operations. Data on these firms is collected and published regularly by the legal press and shows turnover, number of lawyers employed, profits per partner, etc.

There are broad categories into which these law firms are placed. There is a certain amount of debate about which firms should be in which category, and the precise picture changes annually, as some firms will grow faster than others, and the profitability of each firm will clearly vary year on year. There are also fairly frequent mergers between law firms. Therefore, all the categories in this chapter are broadbrush generalisations, and the lists of law firms within them should be viewed as illustrative examples only.

The Lawyer newspaper (which is available online) publishes a report in October every year on the top 200 law firms. The Legal 500 also publishes a directory of law firm profiles and this is also available online (www.legal500.com/books/l500/directory). The general picture at the time of writing is as follows:

Magic Circle

There is a 'Magic Circle' of the most prestigious large international corporate firms which are based in London. The generally accepted view at the moment is that the Magic Circle firms are:

- Allen & Overy (926 UK lawyers)
- Clifford Chance (907 UK lawyers)
- Freshfields Bruckhaus Deringer
- Linklaters (1,100 UK lawyers)
- Slaughter and May (728 UK lawyers).

The figures in brackets are the number of UK fee earners in each firm (comprising partners, assistants, trainees and legal executives) and are taken from The Legal 500 at the date of writing where available, or confirmed directly by the company.

These firms can offer great rewards, with high salaries and high profits per partner. However, the work often involves working long hours in a high-pressure environment. The first four firms have an extensive network of international offices, whereas Slaughter and May instead has strong links with selected overseas firms for international work. In general, many major London law firms have expanded considerably internationally.

Silver Circle

The term 'Silver Circle' of law firms is an informal term, coined by *The Lawyer* in 2005, to refer to those elite firms that are ranked just below the Magic Circle in terms of turnover, but still have considerably higher profits per partner and revenue per lawyer than other firms, together with a premium client base. These firms are also based in London, but most also have an international network of overseas offices.

The Silver Circle is a less settled group than the Magic Circle, but, at the time of writing, the firms within it are generally considered to be:

- Ashurst (600+ UK lawyers)
- Berwin Leighton Paisner (666 UK lawyers)
- Herbert Smith Freehills (626 UK lawyers)
- Macfarlanes (416 UK lawyers)
- Travers Smith (357 UK lawyers).

The City firm SJ Berwin was previously considered to be one of the Silver Circle firms before becoming part of King & Wood Mallesons following a merger in 2013. In 2016, the organisation went into administration.

Although each of these firms fall within the top 50 for total revenue, they are quite spread out in terms of total revenue and are not simply the next biggest firms after the Magic Circle.

The size and the number of international offices for each firm also differ considerably. While companies such as Herbert Smith Freehills, Ashurst and Berwin Leighton Paisner each have a huge number of overseas offices spanning numerous countries, Macfarlanes and Travers Smith each have only two offices abroad. It is important to consider that a global workforce will allow for trainees to experience potential overseas work.

Each of the firms within the Silver Circle has its own set of specialisms, but individual practices still span a wide range of jurisdictions.

American firms

The trend for large leading US law firms to open branches in London has continued apace and the largest US firms are now firmly entrenched in the UK legal market.

The US law firms with significant London branches include:

- Latham & Watkins (250+ UK lawyers)
- White & Case (310 UK lawyers)
- Kirkland & Ellis (182 UK lawyers)
- Skadden, Arps, Slate, Meagher & Flom (118 UK lawyers)
- Weil, Gotshal & Manges (188 UK lawyers)
- Shearman & Sterling (167 UK lawyers).

Other major City firms

In addition to the Magic Circle and Silver Circle, some other large, well-respected City firms are:

- Clyde & Co. (256 UK lawyers in London and 362 across all UK regions)
- CMS (1,310 UK lawyers)
- Dentons (568 UK lawyers)
- Hogan Lovells (806 UK lawyers)
- Norton Rose Fulbright (726 UK lawyers).

Major national and regional firms

If London is not for you, then there are some very large national and regional law firms with a major presence in large cities outside London. They offer the chance to do top-quality work with high-profile clients outside of London. Some of these firms have branches all over the country and many also have offices abroad, or associate offices abroad. These major national and regional law firms include:

- DAC Beachcroft (2,255 UK lawyers)
- DLA Piper (1,000 UK lawyers)

- Eversheds (1,145 UK lawyers)
- Irwin Mitchell (1,355 UK lawyers)
- Pinsent Masons (1,680+ UK lawyers).

What is the work like?

Large law firms tend to offer a comprehensive service to corporate clients, covering areas such as:

- company law
- mergers and acquisitions
- banking/finance law
- capital markets
- commercial litigation
- commercial property law
- competition law
- employment and pensions law
- financial regulatory law
- intellectual property law (i.e. copyright, trademarks and patents).

Work is often undertaken by teams, and the most junior members of the team may have little or no direct contact with the client. A typical area of work for a trainee involves conducting practical legal research or undertaking document checking work known as 'due diligence'.

Large corporate law firms tend to demand extremely high standards from their lawyers, who are well known for working long hours. In exchange, however, these firms offer excellent training and high salaries. They also usually offer good benefits, such as gym memberships, and also in-house catering services, possibly to avoid you ever having to leave your desk!

Most of the larger law firms will sponsor students that they have given training contracts to by paying their course fees for the Legal Practice Course and Graduate Diploma in Law (the postgraduate qualifications necessary to become a solicitor – see Chapter 4 for more details). In most cases, they also offer a maintenance grant of between £4,000 and £9,180 depending on the firm. For more information on the sponsorship and maintenance grants offered by solicitors' firms, visit https://target-jobs.co.uk/career-sectors/law-solicitors.

Starting salaries for trainees in City firms tend to be high, with typical training contract salaries for major law firms in London about £35–£45,000 per annum and many firms offering between £70,000 and £100,000 on qualification. However, for smaller firms outside of London the figures are not as high (see below).

Usually the larger law firms recruit two to three years ahead of when they expect the trainee to start work, and most will have a vacation placement scheme which typically takes place twice yearly, during the Easter and summer periods. As you can imagine, the large law firms tend to be massively over-subscribed. It is not unusual for a lawyer to leave a large law firm once qualified and move to a smaller firm for what is regarded as a better quality of life (i.e. shorter working hours).

Case study

Elizabeth initially won a place at the University of Cambridge to study veterinary medicine after taking A levels in biology, chemistry, physics, Latin and French. However, she quickly realised that she was not enjoying veterinary medicine at all.

'Many of my friends were law students and I had overheard their conversations with great interest; as soon as I got back to Cambridge after my first year, I started to devour law textbooks and finally approached the Law Director of Studies and asked if she would take me on. The central reason behind my choice was interest. Law is more language-based and contains aspects of history, politics, the English language and some philosophy and science, and makes use of writing, problem solving and debating skills.

'I chose to become a solicitor rather than a barrister because certain aspects of the profession – teamwork, more job stability, having a more stable and developed relationship with the client – appealed to me over the corresponding features of the Bar. The career path for solicitors, which allows you to have a job offer by the beginning of your final year of undergraduate study, was also an advantage.'

While at university, Elizabeth did three vacation schemes with large City solicitors' firms and also attended an open day at a fourth. 'I only applied for training contracts with firms I had done a vacation scheme with, as I had had the opportunity to gain a sense of the atmosphere and culture of the office.

'I received offers of training contracts from two of these firms and would have been happy to work for either. However, I chose my current firm (a major corporate US firm) because of the small trainee intake, the entrepreneurial system of picking up work (which I didn't think would suit me at all, but was pleasantly surprised by on the vacation scheme) and most importantly the open, friendly and non-hierarchical culture of the office.'

Elizabeth's first seat for her training contract is in the Regulatory department. 'It is turning out to be a great first seat. I work for around ten or eleven hours a day steadily, and get work from every Regulatory lawyer. In quiet moments I have also picked up some corporate work and some pro bono work. I have only been in the

---

job a few weeks, so I haven't had direct client contact yet, but I have had contact with the firm's lawyers in other offices and with the Financial Conduct Authority. I have been doing a mixture of routine trainee tasks (proofreading, copying and collating documents, telephone notes) with some more exciting research work as well.'

So far, Elizabeth considers the key qualities needed for her job to be: 'attention to detail, enthusiasm, tenacity, the ability to deal with time pressure, organisation and self-motivation.'

Case study

Shidul works as a property lawyer within a national organisation. He currently works in residential conveyancing, which entails all work related to the buying and selling of residential properties.

'When I started college, I was more interested in computing. A few days into my BTEC course, I realised it really wasn't for me. I made the decision to switch to A levels and, as I wasn't entirely sure what I wanted to do, I chose law as one of them as it sounded interesting. It was the A level I found most interesting, and it was on that basis that I opted to apply for law at university.

'Choosing the right university was a difficult process, but I got a lot of support from my college. I wanted to stay somewhere relatively close to home, and decided to study at Nottingham Trent University as their law school had a great reputation as well as being close by! While university was by far one of the best experiences of my life, the work was tough. I had to work so much harder than I anticipated and A levels were nothing in comparison, but if you can complete A levels to a high enough standard to get onto an LLB course, there is no doubt that you can complete it.

'Looking back on my time at university, I wish I had been more clued up on how important it is to acquire legal work experience. You should always be on the lookout for opportunities to apply your learning in a practical environment as this will introduce you to the realities of the real world before you enter a highly competitive job market.

'After graduating from my Legal Practice Course (LPC), I decided to get some legal experience and worked as a case worker at the Citizens Advice Bureau. I only intended on staying for one year, but that quickly turned into three. However, I had no regrets about this as I was now armed with three years' worth of case working experience, which proved to be invaluable when applying for training contracts. I eventually landed a training contract with a local firm and qualified two years later.

'There is no doubt that there were times when I didn't think I would make it, and it takes a lot of determination to stay focused. The route into law can be convoluted, but you will make it if you work hard enough!'

Smaller law firms

These make up the largest number of law firms, and range in size from one solicitor (sole practitioner) to firms with over 50 lawyers. They tend to specialise in areas more relevant to individuals than companies, or have smaller company clients. For example, on most high streets or in smaller town centres you will find at least one small firm dealing with:

- civil litigation (disputes between individuals)
- conveyancing (sale and purchase of property)
- wills, probate and trusts
- employment law
- family law
- criminal law.

Due to the location of their offices, these firms tend to be categorised as high-street firms – but remember that small firms can still offer high-quality corporate work if they have the clients, and every high street is surrounded by small businesses! Do not forget that most large cities will have many small commercial firms dealing with good commercial work, as well as true high-street firms which concentrate more on individuals. Larger firms may take half a dozen trainees a year, whereas the smallest firms may recruit trainees only occasionally as the need arises.

Typically a trainee solicitor in a small firm will have much more client contact from an early stage. You may still be working as part of a team, but normally you will work closely with the supervisor and, upon qualification, you will work autonomously. It is not unusual to have a high degree of responsibility, and even partnership, cast upon you early on.

The financial rewards might not be as high as those in the larger law firms, but smaller law firms tend to offer a different quality of life (i.e. shorter hours) and work that is more related to everyday life. The SRA's minimum required salary for trainees was scrapped in 2014 although employers must pay at least the national minimum wage. Typical trainee starting salaries are around £35,000 in London and £20,000–£25,000 outside of London. Usually small firms do not offer any support with course fees or maintenance. Most people who secure a training contract at a smaller firm will rely on scholarships and bursaries (such as hardship funds and the Law Society Diversity Access Scheme for those who qualify), loans (such as career and professional development loans), part-time work and family support to finance their studies. The support offered varies significantly between firms. It is also worth considering that at some institutions, the LPC and the GDL can be studied part-time over a two-year course, allowing more scope for part-time work and, ultimately, funding.

Once qualified, starting salaries (although they vary depending on the type of firm and its locality) tend to be in the approximate region of £30,000, depending on the area of qualification.

Case study

Peter studied English literature, French and history at A level, after initially considering careers in both journalism and law. 'I decided to study history at the University of Southampton, as that was the subject that I enjoyed the most and I graduated with a 2.i.

'I became more interested in law by speaking to students who were actually studying law, and when I was called to do jury service one summer. Having assessed my strengths and weaknesses, I felt I had the correct skills to become a solicitor.' Peter then took the Graduate Diploma in Law after completing his degree.

'Although I was interested from an academic perspective in being a barrister, I felt I did not have the correct grades to be considered. I also felt that I would enjoy the role of a solicitor more. For example, I really liked the idea of having regular contact with lay people, working in a large team and undertaking non-contentious work.'

Peter made sure that he obtained some work experience while at university: 'I spent two summers working at a small firm in Chancery Lane, where I gained experience in commercial and civil litigation. I also did work experience at a regional firm in Dorset, where I did some more commercial work, and I did work placements at two global firms, where I gained experience in intellectual property and employment. I then did work experience at a high-street firm in West London where I assisted in the conveyancing department.'

Peter is now a conveyancing solicitor at a large, multi-office high-street firm, having started working at the firm as a paralegal. 'When I was interviewed for a paralegal position, I learnt that the firm recruits each paralegal for a year to assess if they have what it takes to be a successful solicitor and many of the partners were products of the paralegal system. I chose my current firm because they have a really good reputation and a lot of offices.

'As a conveyancing solicitor, I currently take on 20 to 25 clients a month. It is said that moving house can be a very traumatic process for an individual and it is really important to have the right people skills where you can successfully reassure a client yet manage their expectations. Although the work is high in volume, it is crucial to remain calm and patient and take the time to explain the legal process in plain English. You must also be a good team player and help enable secretaries and paralegals who work for you to follow routines, and you need to make sure you are approachable and engaging to junior members of staff, regardless of the stress of the job.'

Office-based or in the courtroom?

Traditionally, the work of a solicitor has been predominantly office-based, with some undertaking advocacy work in the lower courts (mainly criminal work in the magistrates' court). This is still mainly the case as, in practice, solicitors can earn more money working in the office than they can waiting around at court for cases to be heard. In addition, the typical hourly charge-out rates for solicitors far exceeds the average charge-out rates of barristers (for example, it is not uncommon for a junior barrister to earn £150 per day for an appearance, whereas trainee solicitors, on average, can earn up to £111 per hour!) – so it is often more economical for the client to instruct a barrister to undertake court work.

Solicitors have been able to obtain the same right to be heard in the higher courts as barristers, known as the higher rights of audience. Once a solicitor has obtained experience of advocacy in the lower courts, they can undertake an additional training course and, upon successful completion of it, take up the higher rights of audience. A number of solicitors have taken this path and 6,823 practising solicitors are now able to represent their clients in court.

What makes a good solicitor?

Because solicitors deal directly with clients, perhaps the most important attribute required to make a good solicitor is excellent communication skills. Solicitors need to bridge the divide between the academic letter of the law and the practicalities of what the client is trying to achieve. The law needs to be explained to the client in terms they can appreciate and understand. Clearly, the demands placed on a solicitor in a large corporate City firm are very different from those placed on a solicitor in a high-street practice dealing with individuals, but all solicitors, wherever they work, will need:

- excellent communication skills
- the ability to cope with time pressure
- attention to detail
- good academic ability
- to be well organised
- the ability to work as a team.

Barristers

One of the complaints about the English legal system is that lawyers are like buses: as soon as one appears, another two or three turn up as well. This impression comes from the fact that solicitors can often employ barristers to give specialist advice or to represent the client in court – so, instead of hiring only one lawyer, the client now has at least two on their hands. This section will outline what barristers do and how their work differs from that of a solicitor.

What is the work like?

Barristers are specialist legal advisors and courtroom advocates: they are lawyers whom other lawyers consult on a specific issue, whether for advice or to make use of their advocacy skills. As suggested in Chapter 1, their work compares to that of consultants or surgeons in the medical profession, whereas the work of a solicitor compares more to that of a GP.

Just as the usual route to a consultant is through a referral from a GP, so the usual route to a barrister is through a solicitor (although there are a few exceptions to this – see Chapter 1, page 3): the Bar is a referral profession, so members of the public cannot generally directly engage a barrister. Solicitors will have good working relationships with barristers and are likely to know or be able to find out the most suitable barrister to deal with a particular case.

Barristers work as individual practitioners: most are self-employed and are responsible for their own caseload. They do, however, form groups, known as chambers, or sets, in which a number of barristers have their offices in the same building and share the administrative expenses of clerks and facilities – but these are not firms. Every chamber has an experienced barrister at its head; there will be a number of other members of varying seniority – permanent members of a set of chambers are known as tenants and temporary members are known as squatters.

Barristers are independent and objective, and will advise a client on the strengths and weaknesses of the case. Unlike solicitors, they automatically have rights of audience (i.e. the right to appear and present a case) in any court in the land. When a barrister qualifies, it is said that they have been 'called to the Bar', which refers to the bar or rail which used to divide the area of the courtroom used by the judge from the area used by the general public: only barristers were allowed to approach the bar to plead (argue) their clients' cases. The term 'barrister' is derived from this usage of bar. Barristers' seniority is measured in terms of their 'years of call' – i.e. how many years it is since they were called to the Bar.

There are two types of barrister: senior counsel and junior counsel. Senior counsel are those senior barristers who have been made Queen's Counsel (QC) as a mark of outstanding ability. This is also known as 'taking silk', which refers to the silk gowns they traditionally wear – thus a senior barrister is often referred to as a silk. A QC is therefore a senior barrister who is normally instructed in serious or complex cases and would usually appear only in the higher courts. Most senior judges once practised as QCs.

Junior counsel is the term used to describe all other barristers who have not been made QCs.

Barristers tend to specialise in particular areas of law, for example civil law, family law, criminal law or immigration law. The work of a civil barrister may be divided into two types: contentious and non-contentious. Contentious work involves cases where litigation is contemplated or a real possibility. Non-contentious work involves advising on matters which have arisen not from a dispute between parties but often from a desire to avoid litigation in the future (for example the drafting of a will, the creation of a trust or advising on the terms of a contract).

Why engage a barrister?

A solicitor might want to engage a barrister for two main reasons. First, to gain an opinion on a matter of law from a person who is an expert or specialist in a particular field; second, to represent the client in court where the solicitor is not allowed to or would prefer a specialist advocate to take on the task. A well-argued case will impress a judge: good cross-examination will impress a jury. A barrister's specialist advocacy skills could make a difference to the outcome of a case.

When a solicitor asks for a barrister's view on a legal point it is known as seeking 'counsel's opinion'; where the barrister is asked to undertake litigation work (for example, disputes between individuals) in court it is known as 'instructing or briefing counsel', though the two expressions are often used loosely today. If an opinion is sought the barrister will be sent the relevant paperwork and will research the area of law and consider the issues before expressing a view as to the merits of the case or what steps to take next. In many cases, barristers are able to give advice on a case simply by looking at the papers. In more complex cases, and certainly cases which go to court, it will usually be necessary to have a conference or consultation with the barrister, typically at the barrister's chambers. If counsel is instructed to act, then the barrister will begin to prepare his or her arguments that will later be used in court. Thus most of a barrister's work will typically be centred on legal disputes. The barrister acts like the old medieval champion: stepping in to fight in the place of the client.

What makes a good barrister?

'You need to have utter confidence in what you are doing – or at least appear to,' says one young barrister. 'You are absolutely vulnerable to the whims of the solicitor. You need to be flexible and robust.' A key skill for a barrister is to persuade, so strong communication skills are high on the list. You also need to be interested in people and business, and to be commercially aware (you will, after all, effectively be running your own small business). Below is a list of skills and qualities you might need:

- strong written and verbal communication skills
- confidence
- energy and drive
- the ability to think on your feet
- flexibility and adaptability
- excellent academic ability
- independence
- interpersonal skills
- meticulousness and ability to master detail
- computer skills
- commercial awareness.

Indeed, the website of the Bar Standards Board (BSB) contains a Health Warning on its website about the difficulties of getting into the barristers' profession (www.barstandardsboard.org.uk).This health warning sets out the qualities that the BSB believes are required of a barrister, which are:

- have a high level of intellectual ability
- are highly articulate in written and spoken English
- can think and communicate under pressure
- have determination and stamina and are emotionally robust.

Who works where?

There are over 12,775 barristers in self-employed independent practice in England and Wales. Although some do a wide variety of legal work, many focus on particular aspects of litigation and the law, specialising in areas such as construction, property, company law, crime, employment, personal injury, taxation, intellectual property and many other areas.

Barristers also work for the Crown Prosecution Service (CPS), the Government Legal Service and magistrates' courts. Some barristers may hardly ever appear in court but spend their time writing opinions and giving advice on complex and difficult areas of law. Most barristers practise from London but many are based in other cities and towns, including Birmingham, Bristol, Cardiff, Leeds, Manchester and Nottingham. All barristers who practise in England and Wales are members of one of the six legal circuits (geographical areas) into which the two countries are divided. The circuits are the areas around which the High Court judges travel to hear the most important cases.

Case study

Claire is a barrister at a large set of chambers in London, specialising in employment law. She was called to the Bar in 1998 and secured a tenancy that same year. She studied for A levels in French, Russian and Latin and then read law (European Option) at Queen's College, Cambridge, spending her third year at the University of Poitiers, France. She got a 2.i in her first year and a First in her final year. She later completed a Masters in Law at Harvard, doing a mixture of antitrust and constitutional law/civil liberties.

Before going to Harvard Claire took a year off. 'After I left college I wasn't sure I wanted to practise law, so I spent a year working for a senior barrister, doing political research and writing speeches on various topics such as human rights and discrimination. I then decided that the Bar probably was for me, so I went to Bar School.'

Claire spent time at a number of solicitors' firms in London during her university summer holidays and found this summer experience to be invaluable not only in giving her CV further credibility but also in helping her decide whether to be a solicitor or a barrister. She initially thought that she wanted to use her languages, and that being a solicitor was the only realistic option if she wanted to live abroad and still practise law as she could work from an overseas office. 'Having done a number of summer placements, however, I realised that I was perhaps not ideally suited to working in a corporate environment. I also wanted the chance, having formulated the arguments in a case, to be able to put them to a judge, and was concerned that if I did not at least try to become a barrister I might always have wondered what it would have been like. Finally, having decided, more or less on the eve of having to fill in the application forms for solicitors' firms, that I wanted to try the Bar instead, I spoke to my dad, who suggested that the Bar was too uncertain and a bad career for a woman. There was no better way of ensuring that his extremely stubborn daughter would choose the Bar.

'While I was at Bar School I spent a lot of my time doing part-time research jobs to cover the cost of the year over and above the scholarship which my Inn had generously given me.' Claire also managed to do five mini pupillages, which were helpful both for confirming that she would like to become a barrister and also for helping her to choose where to apply for a pupillage. 'At the time I was applying for pupillage there were few chambers that were as good as my current chambers in commercial, employment and public law. Also, when I came for a mini pupillage I liked the atmosphere, particularly among the junior tenants. You need to enjoy spending time with your colleagues in every profession, but in view of the size of most chambers, and the slow rate of turnover, you have to be really sure that these are people you would enjoy going for a drink with.'

A typical day or week for Claire varies greatly depending on whether she is in court or in a tribunal – a typical week can involve a conference with a QC about the disclosure of evidence in court; drafting applications; drafting grounds of resistance; settling a long-standing case for an applicant shortly before a hearing; preparing for a judicial review; and preparing a possible injunction. There are also usually various bits and pieces of advisory work, including advising on witness statements for forthcoming hearings. Her hours are irregular and she frequently works in the evenings and at weekends.

Legal executives, paralegals and legal secretaries

Working alongside solicitors in firms are various other legal and support staff who are not fully qualified solicitors, but depending on the level of qualifications they hold may be able to carry out similar work to solicitors.

Legal executives will carry out many of the same tasks as solicitors, usually concentrating on one particular area of the law. They will therefore advise clients, carry out legal research and draft documents.

Paralegals (who may also be known as legal assistants) will work in law firms carrying out more routine legal tasks, including collating documents (for example putting together trial bundles), drafting more straightforward documents and carrying out legal research. Paralegals will often be law graduates who have not moved on to the vocational and professional stages of training. Working as a paralegal can often provide a route into becoming a qualified solicitor. The paralegal profession is currently not formally regulated, which means that it is not necessary to have any formal qualifications to become a paralegal. Nevertheless, paralegals working in law firms are employed by solicitors and therefore regulated by the SRA, although in practice, the SRA usually holds the solicitors responsible if any problems occur with paralegals, as they are meant to be supervised by solicitors at all times. However, owing to the hectic nature of a solicitor's job, increasingly intricate tasks are being delegated to paralegals who are seeing cases through from beginning to end at a much higher frequency. This is especially true of areas where the work involved is fairly repetitive and similar of all cases. The Institute of Paralegals, the leading representative body for paralegals in the UK, publishes a code of conduct, which is a code of best practice. It also administers qualifications for paralegals. For more information see www.theiop.org.

Legal secretaries are basically secretaries who work in law firms – i.e. they give administrative support to solicitors. This will include taking telephone calls from clients, typing up documents and letters to clients, invoicing clients, and preparing and filing legal documents. There are no formal qualifications required to become a legal secretary, but good typing, communication and IT skills are the qualities that any firm employing a legal secretary would look for. There are several bodies offering various training courses for legal secretaries, for example the Institute of Legal Secretaries and PAs (www.institutelegalsecretaries.com).

More paralegals are being recruited to do routine work. This is often seen as a way in for law students hoping to find training contracts.

Case study

Katie began her journey towards a legal career by taking law at A level: 'I chose to study law at A level as it was an area that interested me – my cousin is a barrister and I had done some work experience with him, so was keen to do the A level as a "taster" before university. It was a really enjoyable A level as it was very different to my other subjects, and I enjoyed the problem solving element of it.'

Katie's enthusiasm for the subject meant that, when the time came to choose a degree course, she already knew that she wanted to pursue a legal career: 'I decided that the best way of doing that would be take a law degree as it would enable me to qualify as early as possible. I also liked the fact that the degree included such a wide variety of subjects that it gave me a chance to try different areas of law before specialising.' Katie read law at Southampton University.

'I looked at both the solicitors' and barristers' professions and initially had wanted to be a barrister – I think more because of the "glamour" associated with that and from seeing films and TV programmes featuring them. However, when I was studying, various solicitors and barristers would come to do talks for us and I felt that I was better suited to being a solicitor. I'm not a particularly confident public speaker and we would do mooting contests at university, which were fun but put me off the idea of standing up in court regularly. My work experience at various solicitors' firms also confirmed my preference as I enjoyed the buzz of the offices and the wide range of work involved.'

Katie applied for some vacation schemes during the holidays, but found that these were difficult to get into without some legal work experience first! However, she found other legal work experience during the summer holidays at some fairly small local firms, for one or two weeks at a time: 'This was invaluable as, while it was great studying law, you didn't get a good idea of what it would be like to work in a firm unless you saw it first-hand.'

By the time Katie had completed her Legal Practice Course (LPC), the post-2008 recession was in full swing and competition for training contracts was fierce. Many talented and qualified people were chasing too few places. Therefore, Katie learnt to touch type and found paralegal/secretarial work at a small high-street firm. 'I definitely think the legal experience I gained at this time helped me to get my training contract. The partners at my firm do look at grades when considering applicants for training, but they look just as much at work experience and any insight into the profession that people gain from having some legal work experience. During my training contract interviews, we spoke a lot about the paralegal work I had done so I think that was really important in securing the role.' Katie has also found being able to touch type a useful skill in her legal career: 'Most firms will need someone to at least be a proficient typist, whether they are working as a secretary, paralegal or fee earner, as I still do quite a bit of my own typing!'

Katie is now a conveyancing solicitor at the firm where she did her training contract, a medium-sized regional firm. 'I chose this firm because of its reputation in the local area – I wanted to work at a well-respected firm of a decent size. It had also received awards for training and I therefore felt it would provide me with a good start to my career.

'I qualified into conveyancing which is a busy area. It is a fast-paced job and often stressful, but I enjoy the work as it is intellectually testing at times and varies day to day. I enjoy working with people and have a large amount of client contact, which I really love. I also enjoy working as part of a team and we have a great team of people within our office.

'You need to be well organised, to be able to cope well under pressure and to have excellent communication skills – these are all things that I have developed while on the degree and during my training.

'I have certainly benefitted from all of my legal work experience and my advice to all law students is to just get as much as possible on your CV as it is one thing that can make you stand out from the crowd when applying for training contracts. A lot of the people I went to law school with joined firms straight after the LPC to get some experience and ended up getting their training contracts that way, rather than applying directly for a training contract without any experience.'

The legal profession in Scotland

The main difference in the composition of the legal profession in Scotland is that instead of there being the two separate professions of solicitors and barristers, in Scotland there are solicitors and advocates.

Solicitors

As in England and Wales, solicitors in Scotland give advice on a wide variety of areas of law, with individual solicitors specialising in particular areas. Solicitors in Scotland can represent clients in the Justice of the Peace and Sheriff courts.

Solicitors in Scotland are both represented and regulated by the Law Society of Scotland, which sets standards for the profession, including education and training requirements, and disciplines solicitors where necessary.

Solicitor advocates

Solicitor advocates are experienced solicitors who have extended rights of audience and can also appear in the High Court of Justiciary and the Court of Session. They are members of the Law Society of Scotland and are regulated by that body.

Advocates

Advocates (sometimes referred to as 'counsel') are lawyers that are specifically trained in advocacy, so can represent clients in any Scottish court. They are equivalent to barristers in England and Wales, and the relationship between solicitors and advocates works the same as that between solicitors and barristers in England and Wales, in that advocates are usually instructed through a solicitor instead of being instructed directly by individuals.

Advocates are members of the Scottish Bar, and are regulated and represented by the Faculty of Advocates, which carries out similar functions as the Law Society of Scotland does for Scottish solicitors.

Reform of the legal profession in Scotland

The Legal Services (Scotland) Act 2010 made various changes to the operation of the legal profession in Scotland. It aims to reduce the restrictions on solicitors entering into business relationships with non-solicitors, as the Legal Service Act 2007 has allowed solicitors, barristers and non-lawyers to work together in England and Wales. However, the introduction of so-called alternative business structures in Scotland has been long delayed due to a failure to introduce an appropriate regulatory structure.

> For more information on the legal profession in Scotland see www. lawscot.org.uk and www.advocates.org.uk/about-advocates.

Case study

Laura obtained an undergraduate degree in politics and international relations at the University of Edinburgh before undertaking an undergraduate qualifying law degree at the University of Glasgow and then embarking on the Professional Education and Training Stage.

'I was always interested in political affairs and thoroughly enjoyed my first undergraduate degree. It was during this time that I realised I wanted to pursue a career in law. I feel that doing an undergraduate degree in a different subject was the best possible route for me – it allowed me to develop the necessary skills required to succeed on a degree as rigorous as law as I had developed excellent study and reading habits. As there is no graduate qualification to convert to law in Scotland, I then undertook a second degree which lasted four years. The course itself was extremely demanding and involved a lot of reading, researching and working independently, but it was this academic challenge that I thrived upon.

'Being slightly older and more mature, I really made the most of my time on the law course. I participated in moots and in the university law society activities throughout the duration of my course, and ensured that I took all opportunities to make new contacts. Being proactive meant that I was able to undertake a number of placements in different settings, as well as receive support in applying for competitive vacation schemes. Having a strong application, I was successful in securing a place on a vacation scheme and this provided a real turning point for me.

'After completing my degree, I secured a training contract and there was no doubt that this came down to the breadth of my experiences at an early stage in my career. As well as commitment to academic study, I would really encourage any undergraduates to source placements and gain hands-on experience.

'Though the route to qualification is quite long if you hold an alternative first degree, this shouldn't put people off. Working as a solicitor is stimulating by its very nature and allows you to develop new skills constantly!'

Laura now works as a solicitor in the field of intellectual property law.

The legal profession in Northern Ireland

As in England and Wales, the legal profession in Northern Ireland is divided into the two distinct branches of solicitors and barristers, and these professions have the same roles as in England and Wales. Solicitors in Northern Ireland are represented and regulated by the Law Society of Northern Ireland, and barristers are regulated by the General Council of the Bar of Northern Ireland.

For more information please see: www.lawsoc-ni.org/about-us and www.barofni.com.

4| How to qualify as a lawyer

So now we come to the crucial matter: how do you start on the long road to becoming a lawyer? As there are two distinct branches of the legal profession, there are different training routes for each branch. This chapter will start by looking at how to qualify as a solicitor in England and Wales, followed by an overview of how to qualify as a solicitor in Scotland and Northern Ireland, and will then move on to qualifying as a barrister in each of the three jurisdictions.

Solicitors: England and Wales

It may come as a surprise to learn that there are a number of different routes to qualifying as a solicitor. Most of these are set out in the diagram on page 44 and then described in more detail in the text that follows.

Before university

A levels

A wide range of A levels provide an acceptable grounding for a law degree and there are no specific subject entry requirements to be able to study law at university. The traditional essay-based subjects such as history and English have an obvious appeal: they involve assimilating and analysing information, and a significant amount of writing, which will all be required on a law degree course. Languages may also prove to be very attractive to employers, particularly if you end up working for a firm with offices overseas, and sciences will develop logical thought and application, which are key skills for any lawyer. Many universities do not accept either General Studies or Critical Thinking A levels at all for any of their courses.

The leading Russell Group of 24 top UK universities publishes a document called 'Informed Choices' which provides advice and guidance on choosing A level subjects (www.russellgroup.ac.uk/informed-choices.aspx). This document contains a list of what are termed 'facilitating subjects', which are all the traditional academic subjects:

- maths and further maths
- English (literature)

- physics, chemistry and biology
- history and geography
- modern and classical languages.

The Russell Group universities recommend that potential applicants to these universities choose at least two of their A levels from this list of facilitating subjects. This will keep a wide range of degree courses open to them. Aspiring lawyers should be aware that studying for a law degree involves a considerable amount of reading and research, requiring a high degree of literacy. Therefore, if you choose all maths and science A levels and then wish to study law at university, you may need to be able to demonstrate to your chosen university that you possess the level of literacy and essay-writing skills required on a law degree. This could possibly be done by careful comments in the personal statement on the UCAS form (see Chapter 7, pages 96–105) or perhaps by taking an Extended Project Qualification (EPQ). The EPQ is an additional qualification, which requires you to undertake a self-directed period of research, which is then usually written up in a dissertation-style essay. This can be related either to one of your current A level subjects or to your future career.

Whether or not an aspiring lawyer should choose A level Law seems to cause some controversy. The obvious advantage of taking law at A level is that it will provide you with an introduction to the subject and give you some idea of what studying law is like and whether or not it appeals to you before you have to commit to studying law at university. However, it is also viewed as being a relatively 'soft' A level subject, and could present the problem of students falling into a false sense of security prior to beginning a notoriously rigorous degree. However, research published by the exam board AQA suggests that, in reality, this is generally not the case. Nevertheless, there have been suggestions in the press that A level Law is not favoured by universities, and it is not on the Russell Group list of facilitating subjects.

In March 2014, AQA published a document entitled 'In support of A level Law. Universities don't like A level Law – fact or fiction?'. This document quotes from the A level Law reviews of 2009 and 2010 and also includes comments by law admissions tutors from some top universities, including the University of Cambridge. The conclusion reached was that a large majority of the country's top universities treat A level Law like any other A level, and studying it confers neither an advantage nor a disadvantage when it comes to applying for a law degree. Some even see it as an advantage. The document includes a (long) list of universities which confirmed that A level Law is an acceptable entry qualification for their law courses.

It is still important to bear in mind that A level Law is not a facilitating subject for Russell Group universities. Historically, the London School of Economics and Political Science (LSE) regarded A level Law as a

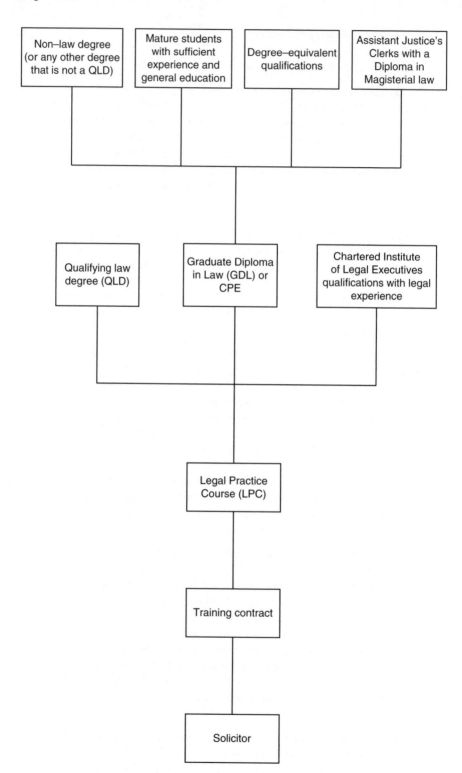

Figure 1: Qualification route for solicitors

non-preferred subject, though their stance on this has changed in recent years and it is now considered as a preferred subject.

If you are hoping to study at a top UK university, then you should follow the Russell Group's advice when choosing A levels and choose at least two subjects from the list of facilitating subjects. If you wish to study A level Law, you should also choose at least two traditional subjects from the list to study alongside it. With all of your A level choices, it is important to choose subjects because you think you will enjoy them and they will play to your strengths. You should not choose law because this is the subject you wish to pursue at degree level, as no university stipulates that it is a requirement. To be on the safe side, you should also take the following steps:

- if you already have a university in mind, check with the admissions section of its website to determine its specific entry requirements are and, if you wish to take law (or any other non-facilitating subject), whether or not it will be considered
- if you are already studying for your A levels but have not yet chosen which universities you would like to apply to, then do your research before applying so that you know which universities will accept your combination of A level subjects.

Access to Higher Education courses

If you are a mature student who missed out on completing your secondary education, and cannot satisfy university entry requirements, Access to HE courses are designed to help you move into higher education and on to degree-level studies. Most access courses are delivered in further education colleges (although some are available at certain universities) and are available across England and Wales. The courses can be taken in a range of different subjects and lead to the Access to Higher Education Diploma, which is widely recognised by universities.

To find out more about Access to HE courses, visit the Access to Higher Education website (www.accesstohe.ac.uk), which contains further information on the Diploma and a link to a database of further education colleges offering Access courses.

Some employers will particularly welcome applicants who have had some 'life experience' in other fields before starting their legal career and the skills and qualities that more mature applicants offer can be much valued. This will be the case more for some employers than others (the civil service and teaching profession are good examples), although all employers must disregard age in their recruitment decisions to avoid breaking anti-age-discrimination laws. However, you should research the legal career you are interested in carefully before embarking on the expensive and time consuming training to becoming a lawyer.

Academic stage of training

Law degree

Many universities offer law degrees, and these vary to some extent in style and content – for example:

- some are more traditional and 'academic' in approach
- some are slightly more vocational in outlook
- some enable you to obtain a joint degree (e.g. law and languages, law and politics, law and accountancy).

This variety gives you the opportunity to choose the degree which best suits your skills and interests – but if you have any intention of qualifying as a solicitor, you should ensure that your degree is recognised by the Solicitors Regulation Authority (SRA) as a qualifying law degree (QLD) – see Chapter 6, page 84 for details. The SRA maintains a list of certain institutions and the degrees they offer that are recognised as QLDs, so it is easy to check whether your preferred degree is on the list. Having a QLD means that you have studied the subjects which the SRA considers to be the core foundation subjects for any lawyer.

These are:

- obligations (including contract, restitution and tort law)
- criminal law
- public law (including constitutional law, administrative law and human rights law)
- land (or property) law
- equity and the law of trusts
- law of the European Union.

The Law Society stipulates that, for a degree to constitute a QLD, the study of legal subjects must account for not less than two years out of a three- or four-year course of study (i.e. 240 credits in a 360 or 480 credit degree programme). At least half of a normal three-year degree course (i.e. 180 credits) must be spent on the foundation subjects listed above. Some study of legal subjects must also take place in the final year of the course. The SRA also stipulates that the teaching methods must allow students to acquire knowledge and understanding of the fundamental doctrines and principles which underpin English law. A detailed list of QLDs and their providers can be found on the SRA website (www.sra.org.uk/students/courses/qualifying-law-degree-providers.page).

Once you begin looking for a training contract (see below), you will discover that many firms will expect you to have either a First or 2.i degree. You will need to work hard right from the outset of your degree to maximise your chances of getting a training contract with the firm of your choice.

Non-law degrees: the Graduate Diploma in Law (GDL)

What do you do if your degree is in a subject other than law and, during or on completion of your studies, you decide that you wish to qualify as a lawyer? In this case, you would need to obtain an additional post-graduate qualification, which is usually known as the GDL – although some universities and colleges (and indeed the SRA) still refer to it by its former name: the Common Professional Examination (CPE). This qualification is accepted by both the Bar Council and the SRA, so, subject to the need to apply for vocational training places as early as possible (see below), you could start the GDL without having decided whether you eventually intend to qualify as a solicitor or as a barrister, and then make your decision during the course of your studies.

The GDL is a condensed programme of study, usually comprising a one-year full-time course offered at around 50 universities and law schools across England and Wales. Many of the same institutions offer the GDL on a part-time basis over two years for added flexibility. Part-time online distance learning programmes are also available through some institutions, allowing students to work while studying. As with qualifying law degrees, the SRA maintains a list of all institutions that offer the GDL (available at www.sra.org.uk/students/conversion-courses/cpe-gdl-providers.page).

Application for a full-time GDL course is made via the Central Applications Board (the CAB), which runs an online system similar to UCAS (see Chapter 7), acting as a hub for all full-time applications for the GDL and LPC (see below). Up to three different institutions can be applied to at once. There are no application deadlines for the CAB, which simply recommends that candidates should apply at their 'earliest convenience', but it does advise you to check on the individual course providers' web-sites for application closing dates as they may not accept late applications. Applications for part-time or distance learning GDL courses are made direct to the institution(s) of your choice. Applicants must register on their website (www.lawcabs.ac.uk) and there is a £15 registration fee.

The current cost of a full-time GDL ranges from around £4,000 to around £10,000. You should check what the course fee includes – for example, some providers will include the cost of all books and materials within their fees, whereas others will expect you to pay for these direct. You should also investigate the amount of contact time offered by the different course providers. Remember that you often get what you pay for, so do not necessarily opt for the most inexpensive course. Try to talk to some students who are currently studying or have previously studied at the institution you are interested in to find out whether they were happy with the course. You should also consider where you would like to do your training contract, as certain law firms favour specific law schools. For more information on funding the GDL, and the choice of institution for the GDL and LPC, please see below.

Case study

Ben followed an interesting route into the field of law. When applying for university, Ben was eager to study law, but was also keen to study in Scotland, where he was born.

'In a nutshell, my route into law wasn't conventional, but it was by no means atypical. As with all businesses, law firms look for different people with different skill sets, and many of my colleagues have done "something else" before coming to law.

'Not wanting to commit to a decision between Scottish or English law at a relatively young age, and therefore effectively deciding where I would live and work, I decided to study English, in Scotland, with a view that I would study law at postgraduate level. After four years at Edinburgh, I couldn't afford to continue being a student straight away, and I was keen to take a break from studying. I had also been offered a professional singing job and the offer was too good to turn down!

'Having then decided that singing wasn't what I wanted to do as a full-time job, I went to work in London for a medium-sized recruitment firm as a consultant. In many ways this was the perfect first job as, unlike law, accountancy or parts of banking, I didn't need to take any additional exams or undergo a huge amount of formal training. From day one I had responsibility for winning business and maintaining relationships with clients, which I really enjoyed. Although this was an extremely tough job with sales targets, "cold calling" and very long hours, it was a brilliant way of learning the "nuts and bolts" of business processes and day-to-day work. After 18 months of recruiting, my dad was diagnosed with cancer and I moved home to Somerset to look after him. It was at that point I was able to rethink what I really wanted to do and I decided to go back to university!

'I started my GDL at BPP University Law School in Bristol, chosen for its close proximity to home and its stance as the second city for law in the UK, with many top firms either basing themselves or maintaining a regional office there. The GDL was tough, but incredibly useful in providing a thorough grounding in the fundamentals that underpin law. During that year I applied for training contracts with law firms and was lucky enough to be offered a place at Burges Salmon in Bristol. I believe that I was successful in securing this training contract as I was able to show commitment to a role that requires working long hours, forming good relationships with clients, meeting targets and winning business. It is also important to research what makes a law firm different – you need to consider their culture, the work that they do and who they act for in your application. They need to see that you are serious about a career in law – while I didn't really have much work experience in the field, I was able to show a genuine interest at interview and prove that I was determined for the difficult journey ahead.

'While I wait to start my LPC in Bristol in September 2019, I am working as a paralegal in the field of clinical risk (medical negligence), which I find extremely interesting.'

Non-graduate route

If you do not possess a degree, there are still a number of options available to you. You may apply to the SRA for a certificate of academic standing which will allow you to apply for the GDL course. This is granted by the SRA if it is satisfied that you hold other academic or vocational qualifications that it considers to be equivalent to a degree. Briefly, the situations where this may be possible include the following.

- **Mature students** – if you have a considerable amount of experience (normally at least 10 years) or have shown exceptional ability in an academic, professional, business or administrative field and have been educated to at least A level standard, and have a good command of both spoken and written English, the SRA may issue a certificate to allow you to take up a place on the GDL course.
- **Assistant Justices' Clerks** – clerks who have gained a Diploma in Magisterial Law are usually eligible to take the GDL, and may even be granted exemptions from some of the papers.
- **Chartered legal executives** – those already working in the legal sector, for example as a paralegal, could take the Chartered Institute of Legal Executives' examinations during a period of qualifying employment. These qualifications are recognised by the SRA as being equivalent to a law degree and therefore enable you to progress to the next stage of training, the LPC (see below) without obtaining a degree.
- **Degree-level qualifications** – these may include professional accountants' or surveyors' qualifications.

More information on the non-graduate route to qualification is contained in the Academic Stage Handbook, which is available on the SRA website. If in any doubt, you should contact the SRA, whose staff will be able to give you advice on your particular circumstances.

Vocational stage of training

Legal Practice Course (LPC)

Following completion of the academic stage of training, aspiring solicitors must complete an LPC at one of around 35 universities and law schools across England and Wales. The LPC can be completed over one year full-time or two years part-time (in a variety of formats including day, evening or weekend study patterns). The current cost ranges from around £11,700 to around £16,000 for the full-time course. The yearly fees are less for the part-time courses.

The LPC is made up of a combination of compulsory and elective modules. The compulsory modules cover the subjects and skills in the core practice areas, including business law and practice, property law and practice as well as litigation, and these must be covered irrespective of where the LPC is studied. You will also take three elective modules which you will be able to choose from the range offered by your chosen course provider. Different institutions offer different elective subjects, so when you apply for the LPC, you should make sure that you choose courses that offer the elective modules that you are interested in studying and pursuing as a career.

The larger solicitors' firms that offer help with fees for the LPC (see page 54) often only do so if you study for it at one of their preferred course providers and take the optional modules that are most relevant to their areas of practice. For example, if you intend to work in the City as a corporate lawyer, you will need to take commercial law options. BPP University has strong ties to the leading firms in the City and is the exclusive course provider for trainees from over 50 leading law firms. The University of Law is the preferred training provider for over 30 more law firms. You need to make sure that you take the LPC at the institution preferred by the law firm at which you would like to work.

The LPC is very different from the academic stage of training: it is based on legal practice rather than theory, and you will spend a lot more time in small groups with other students. The skills content of the course means you will experience much more 'learning by doing'.

As with the GDL, applications for a full-time LPC course must be made via the Central Applications Board (www.lawcabs.ac.uk). Again, the CAB does not have application deadlines for the LPC, but you should check with the institutions individually to see whether they have their own application deadlines. Applications for part-time courses are made direct to the institution(s) of your choice.

Exempting degree

The idea behind the exempting degree is to combine the academic and vocational stages of training. At the time of writing, only six exempting law degrees are on offer. The universities that offer these include:

- Huddersfield University, Law (Exempting) Master of Law and Practice MLP
- Northumbria University, LLB Law Hons with Masters (Exempting)
- Pearson College London (validated by the University of Kent), M. Law Legal Professional Practice
- University of Central Lancashire, M. Law
- University of South Wales, M. Law, Legal Practice
- University of Westminster, Solicitors Exempting LLB Honours.

More information about exempting law degrees can be found on the SRA website (www.sra.org.uk/students/exempting-law-degrees.page). The degrees are four years long and, on completion of your studies, you'll be deemed to have the equivalent of both a QLD (see page 46) and the LPC. The obvious attraction of the exempting degree can be the funding arrangements.

Training contract

The final stage of your route to qualification as a solicitor is the training contract. This is (usually) two years of on-the-job training with a firm or other organisation which has been authorised by the SRA to take trainee solicitors. The purpose is to enable you to understand the practical implications of the law as well as developing your legal skills. The SRA requires you to gain experience in at least three distinct areas of law during your training contract and to further develop your legal skills while doing so. You should spend at least three months working in each of these areas. You will also have to complete the Professional Skills Course (PSC), which includes further training and some assessment in legal skills. Your firm or employer is expected to support you through this process and must pay your fees and reasonable travel expenses.

Depending on the sort of firm you want to go to for your training contract, you may need to apply up to three years in advance of your possible start date. This is certainly the case with the large City and national corporate and commercial firms, which will be recruiting as you are entering either the penultimate or the final year of your degree studies or starting your GDL. The application deadlines vary from firm to firm – some recruit earlier than others and some only have relatively short windows in which they will accept applications in any one year. Most recommend applying early. Other firms and organisations will recruit you as you are completing your LPC, with a view to an immediate start, so it is also common for students to start their LPC without knowing if they have a training contract to go to at the end of the course. There is a voluntary Code of Good Conduct for the recruitment of trainee solicitors, which represents good practice in legal recruitment. Law firms are not obliged to follow this Code, but most will in practice. The Code is available on the Law Society's website and specifies, among other things, that the opening date for training contract applications must not be earlier than the penultimate year of your undergraduate study. You cannot accept or decline any offers before 15 September in your final undergraduate year.

You can complete your training contract on a part-time basis and you can also combine your training contract with attendance on a part-time LPC. If you have considerable previous work experience in a legal environment, then you may be eligible for a reduction in the length of your training contract of up to six months, but this will depend on whether your employer supports your request. Any application has to be made to the SRA.

Competition for training contracts is fierce. Following the advice in this book should put you in the best possible position to obtain a training contract. You should also consider your A level choices carefully and obtain the best grades you can, as well as considering your choice of university carefully – there is some evidence that the top firms still look to what they perceive as the 'good' universities for their trainees. Finally, enrol on some vacation schemes and try hard to obtain some relevant work experience (see Chapter 5 for more details).

Students enrolling on the LPC (2015/2016)	5,952
New training contracts started (2015/2016)	5,728

Table 2: Competition for solicitors' training contracts

Proposed changes to the route of qualification

The SRA have recently published their proposals to modify the route into qualifying as a solicitor by introducing the Solicitors Qualifying Examination (SQE) in 2020. The SQE will provide a centralised assessment route and eradicate the variable and inconsistent pass rates of the LPC due to differences between providers. Using the current system, it is difficult to ensure that all new solicitors are assessed equally and rigorously. At present, the LPC is an expensive gamble: aspiring solicitors pay up to £15,000 with no guarantee of securing a training contract, with prices set to increase further. As a result, introducing the SQE will minimise the cost of training.

The SQE would be divided into two main components. Stage 1 would be completed before the work-based experience, with Stage 2 being completed following its conclusion. It is likely that there will be two periods of assessment per calendar year, with new solicitors having six years to complete both stages of the assessment (see Table 3 on the opposite page).

Stage 1	Stage 2
Prior to undertaking work-based training, candidates will complete six Functional Legal Knowledge Assessments, covering: ● Principles of Professional Conduct, Public and Administrative Law, and the Legal Systems of England and Wales ● Dispute resolution in Contract or Tort ● Property Law and Practice ● Commercial and Corporate Law and Practice ● Wills and the administration of Estates and Trusts ● Criminal Law and Practice They must also undertake one Practical Legal Skills Assessment: ● Legal Research and Writing	Following the completion of a period of work-based training, five Practical Legal Skills Assessments are completed in two practice contexts of the candidate's choice from the following: ● Criminal Practice ● Dispute resolution ● Property ● Wills and the administration of Estates and Trusts ● Commercial and Corporate Practice Candidates must therefore undertake a total of ten assessments in the following areas: ● Client interviewing ● Advocacy/persuasive oral communication ● Case and matter analysis ● Legal research and written advice ● Legal drafting

Table 3: Solicitors Qualifying Examination (SQE) stages

As well as passing the SQE, new solicitors would also need to attain an appropriate degree or apprenticeship, undertake around two years of workplace training and meet the appropriate candidate and suitability requirements.

Appropriate work-based training could be obtained in a variety of ways, including formal training contracts, working in a law clinic, undertaking an apprenticeship, working as a paralegal or through a placement as part of a sandwich degree. In each instance, a supervising solicitor would be required to sign a declaration that the student had the opportunity to develop the competencies in the Statement of Solicitor Competence.

Finalisation of the SQE will follow, with the most up-to-date information accessible on the SRA website (www.sra.org.uk/home/hot-topics/Solicitors-Qualifying-Examination.page).

Funding your qualification

Qualifying as a solicitor, therefore, has become an expensive business and it's not unusual for students to find themselves in tens of thousands of pounds of debt at the end of their LPC. So, what are your options?

Sponsorship

Most of the larger firms will sponsor you through the LPC and possibly the GDL if you have secured your training contract before commencing the course. The sponsorship will cover the cost of the GDL/LPC course fees and usually a contribution towards your living expenses as well. You'll need to check whether the firms that interest you would offer sponsorship of this kind. Firms providing sponsorship deals often do so on the proviso that you take your LPC at their preferred university or college. This is so that they can make sure that you study the subjects that they will need you to know about once you start working for them.

Law Society Diversity Access Scheme

The Law Society has a Diversity Access Scheme (DAS), which is aimed at students from disadvantaged backgrounds or those who face exceptional obstacles to qualification. Applicants must meet several of the listed criteria, which include aspects such as:

- attended a non-fee paying school
- part of the first generation of the family to have attended higher education
- recipient of free school meals during compulsory-aged education
- exceptional circumstances relating to gender, ethnicity, sexual orientation, health, disability, educational or other personal obstacles.

Its purpose is to increase social diversity in the legal profession. The DAS offers payment of LPC course fees, plus the provision of work experience and a professional mentor.

The scheme is, however, extremely limited: in 2016, the Law Society offered ten standard DAS awards, as well as one DAS Plus award, which also guarantees a training contract at a national law centre. Applications are typically accepted between February and April each year, and students are required to reflect on their financial situation, their desire to become a solicitor, the contributions they could make, current affairs and their work experience to date. Competition for awards is keen and applicants must have a confirmed place on the LPC.

More details are available on the Law Society's website (www.law society.org.uk/law-careers/diversity-access-scheme).

Career development loans

Once you get to the LPC stage of training, you may be eligible for a career development loan up to the value of £10,000. These are deferred repayment loans offered by certain banks to fund vocational training courses. The Government pays the interest on the loan while you are studying and you repay the loan once you start working. For more information see www.gov.uk/career-development-loans.

Access funds and scholarships

These are available at some universities offering the LPC. Access funds may be available at publicly funded colleges and are discretionary awards aimed at assisting with your living costs if you are experiencing financial hardship. Scholarships may be awarded by any of the universities or colleges offering the LPC to students with particularly good academic backgrounds. Details are available direct from your institution of study.

Payment by instalments

Some institutions where you can take the LPC course offer the option to pay by instalments. You should check the institutions' individual websites for details.

Charities and grant-making trusts

Some grant-making trusts and charities may offer financial assistance to those seeking to qualify as a lawyer. You should search online to see whether there are any such bodies in the area where you live and, if there are, check whether you meet their criteria for an award. These are usually very specific, so that eligibility is extremely limited.

Study part-time

More and more students are completing their professional training part-time, mostly due to the lack of financial support. This will enable you to work part-time to help support yourself. You should, however, make sure that you allow yourself enough time to study so that you pass the course.

Funding: conclusion

When you are looking for sources of funding, remember:

- do your research
- plan ahead
- read the criteria for any grant/award you are applying for very carefully and make sure you can demonstrate that you meet them
- don't be put off – you're hoping to train to be a solicitor so try to come up with a good case for yourself
- be realistic.

Case study

Uthman recently completed a law degree at the University of Birmingham and is now pursuing a career in international arbitration.

'I really wasn't sure what I wanted to do as a career during my A levels, but I opted to study law on the basis that I had a genuine love of reading and thoroughly enjoyed critical thinking. I knew that these were fundamental aspects of studying law and knew that securing a solid law degree would allow me to acquire a huge range of transferable skills which would be beneficial despite not having a defined idea of the route I would follow after graduation.

'The sciences I studied at A level ensured that I was scientifically literate, and taught me to be thorough in my approach to study. Studying history was by far the biggest help in preparing me for a degree in law, though: constantly writing long essays and having to think analytically while retaining vast quantities of information was very much in line with what was expected of me as an undergraduate law student. In addition, studying psychology was helpful in allowing me to practice critical thinking. Being able to think philosophically was incredibly useful, and I would encourage all prospective applicants to read widely, and watch and participate in debates as much as possible. Reading the work of authors such as George Orwell encouraged me to consider political issues and societal changes.

'I covered these areas in my personal statement, but was unsuccessful in my application to LSE as I did not demonstrate a thorough understanding of what the course entailed. This really demonstrates the importance of trying to secure legal work experience and conducting specific wider reading for discussion in your personal statement and at interview.

'I found the course itself particularly tough. Much of the first year involved learning vast quantities of information, long hours of study and real commitment. In the second year, I found that I really enjoyed the jurisprudence module. I then went on to study controversial areas such as counter-terrorism law and international human rights, which were incredibly engaging. It involved thinking deeply rather than just learning facts, and undertaking a research dissertation was fascinating in terms of the amount of information I learned and the research skills that I developed.

'I am now pursuing a career in international arbitration following careful consideration of my options. This was predominantly influenced by my internship. Securing internships and work experience placements are crucial in developing the necessary practical skills required in law and establishing areas of interest. It is also an international career, with the potential to travel. I am currently in the process of applying for an LLM in London and America, as well as a training contract. I am confident that my internship will have provided me with the necessary skills and anecdotes required for a successful application.'

Solicitors: Scotland

As outlined in Chapter 2, the legal system in Scotland differs from that of England and Wales and Northern Ireland, and so does the qualification route. This section aims to summarise the process of qualifying as a solicitor in Scotland.

Briefly, the route to qualification involves studying for a four-year law degree at a Scottish university and then proceeding to the vocational training stage. There is no equivalent of the GDL in Scotland, so it is slightly more difficult to become a lawyer if your degree is in a subject other than law, as this necessitates taking a two-year accelerated law degree after your first degree. Further details on qualifying in Scotland are available on the Law Society of Scotland's website (www.lawscot. org.uk/members/business-support/recruitment-guidance/overview-of-the-route-to-qualification).

Academic stage

Law degree

It is possible to study a Bachelor of Law degree (LLB) at the following Scottish universities:

- University of Aberdeen
- University of Abertay
- University of Dundee
- University of Edinburgh
- Edinburgh Napier University
- Glasgow Caledonian University
- University of Glasgow
- Robert Gordon University
- University of Stirling
- University of Strathclyde.

More detailed information about the content of the courses can be obtained from the law schools at each of the universities' wesbites.

The law degrees are honours degree courses, which in Scotland are studied over four years. Students who already have a degree in another subject can apply for a two-year accelerated degree.

A law degree from an English university will not be accepted as a QLD in Scotland, and vice versa. However, if you have qualified in England, Wales, Northern Ireland or other parts of the European Union, there are transfer tests available in order to requalify in Scotland. Information on how to convert qualifications from a different country (e.g. if you qualified in England but want to practise in Scotland) can be found by visiting the websites of the law societies and bar councils for each country.

The non-graduate route

Alternatively, there is a non-degree route where someone who has been working as a full-time pre-Diploma trainee with a qualified solicitor in Scotland for three years can take the Law Society of Scotland's examinations and then proceed to the vocational stage of training in the same way as a law graduate. This route is known as the Pre-PEAT Training Contract and LSS exams, and, according to the Law Society of Scotland, is followed by between 10 and 20 people each year. For more information please see www.lawscot.org.uk/members/business-support/recruitment-guidance/overview-of-the-route-to-qualification.

Vocational stage

Diploma

After completion of the LLB degree all aspiring Scottish solicitors are required to take the Diploma in Professional Legal Practice (DPLP) which is also known as the Professional Education and Training Stage 1 (PEAT 1). It is usually taught full-time over one academic year, though some two-year part-time courses are also available. These can be studied at:

- University of Aberdeen
- University of Dundee
- University of Edinburgh
- University of Glasgow
- Robert Gordon University
- University of Strathclyde.

The DPLP is the equivalent of the LPC in England and Wales, in that the course has been designed to teach the practical knowledge and skills necessary for the working life of a solicitor. The focus is highly practical and skills-based. To obtain a place on the diploma course, applicants would need to have passed all of the Law Society of Scotland's 'professional subjects' in their LLB (or Law Society examinations). Applications are made direct to the universities offering the course.

Training contract

After successful completion of the degree (or non-graduate route) and diploma, you need to serve a two-year post-diploma training contract (Professional Education and Training Stage 2, or PEAT 2) with a practising solicitor in Scotland. This can be served with solicitors in private practice, the Crown Office, or local authorities and certain public bodies. The training contract is very similar to that in England and Wales, giving trainees the chance to put into practice what they have learnt at university. At the end of the two years, if the training contract has been successful then the trainee is qualified and can apply for a full practising certificate. As in England and Wales, competition for training contracts is intense and there are now fewer trainee roles available for a similar number of students passing the DPLP. A good academic profile is therefore important and the benefits of having obtained some work experience, particularly in the legal sector, cannot be over-estimated.

Case study

Stewart works as a solicitor in Scotland at an accident claim and injury firm. His route into law was long-winded and undoubtedly tough, but his perseverance paid off!

'I grew up in quite a rough part of Edinburgh, the kind of area where aspirations are thin on the ground and very few prosper due to lack of hope, money and opportunity. In short, I left school with no qualifications. I was told by my teachers at a very early age that I would not amount to much in life and I believed them. I eventually left school with nothing to show for my time there and a paper round that yielded £7 per week. I later took up a part-time job in a local music store but despite my best efforts, no full-time roles became available for me. I had a friend who worked in a solicitors' firm as an Office Junior and one day, he mentioned that there was a position available. I applied but was once again met with rejection, until I eventually received my stroke of luck – the person who had taken the position initially left after just a few weeks, so the job was mine!

'The solicitors' firm was a small trade union firm where I worked as an Office Junior in the Filing Department. I loved it – one of the perks of working for a small firm is that it feels as though you are working with a big family! From filing I moved onto data processing, before eventually being promoted to the role of Executive in Information Technology, which was a position I maintained for a number of years. To earn some extra money, I took on a part-time job as a bar man. It was while working in the bar after a day at the office that I had a bit of an epiphany – I was working with the next generation of lawyers who were not much smarter than me. I decided to go for broke and see whether I could qualify as a lawyer myself.

'I contacted the Law Society to find out what was required and it was contingent on a lot of things coming together: primarily, consent from my employers, attending night school to get higher academic grades, then passing nine exams before applying to do the diploma. I then approached one of the partners to gauge his views and, like many other times in my life, he told me he didn't think I was up to it. I was deflated somewhat but not deterred, and instead approached the most senior partner in the firm. To my surprise, he completely supported my decision and told me to return after I'd completed my exams so that I could talk to the partners. He was true to his word, and the company then supported me through the Law Society exams while allowing me to work as a pre-diploma trainee.

'This was a tough undertaking and I had to give up a lot – football, seeing my friends and family – as it meant long working hours, seven days a week, for four years. I was handed a syllabus but, other than that, no direction at all – there were no lectures or tutors, just huge piles of books! One of the stipulations from the Law Society was that all exams had to be passed within four sittings. By the end of the fifth year of studying, I had passed every exam other than the nemesis of taxation, in which I was about to undertake my fourth attempt at the exam. Having done so, I received a call to say I had failed. I was heartbroken and the Law Society bluntly told me I was out of options. I contacted directly each of the universities offering the diploma, but despite my pleas, they all closed the door. A glimmer of hope came from Alan Barr at the University of Edinburgh, who suggested I sit the taxation exam at undergraduate level the following term and, if I passed, he would allow me to study the diploma. I took him up on his offer and really couldn't believe how easy the exam was – the lecturers were incredibly helpful and I passed the exam, allowing me to ultimately qualify as a solicitor.'

Solicitors: Northern Ireland

The system for qualifying as a solicitor in Northern Ireland is different again from those in England, Wales and Scotland. Below is a brief summary, but further details can be obtained from the Law Society of Northern Ireland's website (www.lawsoc-ni.org/becoming-a-solicitor).

Academic stage

The usual route to qualification as a solicitor in Northern Ireland begins with a law degree. This must be considered by the Law Society of Northern Ireland to be a 'recognised law degree', and must contain eight core subjects. These include:

- law of evidence
- land law

- European law
- equity
- constitutional law
- law of tort
- law of contract
- criminal law.

Further details of what constitutes a recognised law degree, and a list of recognised law degrees and the universities offering them, are available on the website of the Institute of Professional Legal Studies, part of Queen's University, Belfast (the 'Institute'). This list of recognised law degrees contains many from English and Welsh universities, as well as some in the Republic of Ireland, so this part of the route to qualification does not have to be taken in Northern Ireland. Degrees in Scottish law are not, however, recognised.

Students with non-law degrees can also qualify as a solicitor by first taking the Masters in Law at Queen's University, Belfast. This is an accelerated, fast-track programme that lasts two years when studied full time.

There is also an alternative, non-law degree route available. Typically, these individuals must have qualifications that render them suitable for consideration (i.e. the same as those required for a place at Queen's University, Belfast), and would usually be over 30 years of age. Please visit the website of the Law Society of Northern Ireland (www.lawsoc-ni. org/becoming-a-solicitor) for further details.

Vocational stage and apprenticeship

The vocational training to become a solicitor in Northern Ireland (the Postgraduate Diploma in Legal Practice) is undertaken at the Institute. All applicants applying for the diploma must sit an entrance exam in the December before they wish to commence the course (known colloquially as the 'Institute exam'). Applications must be submitted to the Institute by 15 November in the relevant year. The main difference from the system in England and Wales is that applicants must have already found a master (a solicitor with whom the applicant proposes to serve his/her on-the-job training, known as the apprenticeship) by the time they apply for the vocational course. The vocational course is then combined with the apprenticeship. Finding a master can be a difficult and competitive process.

The apprenticeship is similar to a training contract in England and Wales, in that it will last for two years for trainees who completed the traditional qualification route. However, in order to combine it with the vocational training, each year is structured as follows.

- September to December: spent in-office.
- January to December: spent at the Institute of Professional Legal Studies (but returning to master's office during vacations).
- January to August: spent in-office.

Once a trainee has passed all the relevant examinations and completed their apprenticeship, they can apply to be enrolled as a solicitor of the Court of Judicature in Northern Ireland and apply for a Practising Certificate. A restricted practising certificate is issued for the first two or three years, meaning that newly qualified solicitors can only practise as employees.

For more information on qualifying as a solicitor in Northern Ireland, please see www.lawsoc-ni.org/becoming-a-solicitor.

Case study

Andrew is a solicitor at the Law Society of Northern Ireland. He followed a relatively straightforward route into law and has amassed a range of experience in different areas of law through his route to qualification and following graduation.

'At the age of 17, I took on a month-long placement at my family's solicitors' firm in my home town of Coleraine. It was a typical small country practice with three solicitors dealing with all different types of work. I experienced a variety of cases including criminal, conveyancing, personal injury, Children Order, family and administration of estates. It also gave me the opportunity to sit in on police interviews, court hearings and meet the local judge in chambers. This was my first real introduction into the field of law.

'Shortly afterwards, I commenced my A level studies in economics, maths and politics, securing grades ABB. This was sufficient to get me into Queen's University, Belfast, to study law. I decided upon a law degree because I thought it was a good general degree to have. I did not have any burning desire to do anything in particular so was essentially trying to cover my bases! I knew I would pick up a wealth of transferable skills that would be beneficial regardless of what I decided to do after graduating.

'The degree was very much the traditional three-year law degree that covered each of the core areas. While I was academically capable, I found the course quite dry and still hadn't really pinned down what I wanted to do with my life. At the end of my degree, I worked for a summer in an accountants' firm while also putting in my application to the Institute of Professional Legal Studies (IPLS) in Belfast. The entrance exam to the IPLS at that stage was a very practical exam that did not depend upon your detailed knowledge

---

of law, but was based more on a comprehension-type exercise. This suited me and I managed to get an excellent exam mark.

'The IPLS works on the basis that you must obtain a masters degree, so I got a place in a solicitors' firm in Belfast. The term commenced with a full-time placement in the office followed by lessons at the IPLS. The course itself was a mixture of lectures and small group study sessions. It also incorporated practical exercises, such as mock bail applications and client interviews. This course offered a much more practical introduction to the day-to-day work of a solicitor than the undergraduate degree course.

'I worked in corporate and commercial law for nine months after qualifying. I did not particularly enjoy this type of work so I moved to another firm to do property and private client work. This work was much more to my liking and I stayed there for several years until I joined the Law Society. During my time at the property firm, I became a member of the Society of Trust and Estate Practitioners.

'My experience in private practice was challenging, particularly on the property side. With the property crash from July 2007, there were a number of rounds of redundancies which I thankfully managed to avoid, mostly due to being the only solicitor in the firm who did private client work. I acted for a large number of property developers, some of whom went bust during those years so there was very little work around. My private client work basically supported my property work during this time. The commercial realities of life in private practice were reinforced at this time. Billing, outstanding costs and cashflow became even more vital than previously.

'I moved to the Law Society to deal with all non-contentious work. I am secretary to the Conveyancing & Property Committee, Non-Contentious Business Committee and the Human Rights & Equality Committee, among other duties. The work is challenging but interesting. In particular, I am currently dealing with the review of the Home Charter Scheme (the Northern Irish equivalent of the QCS which has been in place since 1994); this means servicing four additional sub-committees and dealing with all the technical drafting that is produced. The most difficult but most interesting part of this is the review of the General Conditions of Sale (the NI standard property contract). I also give seminars to our members on a variety of subjects. I will have done 15 seminars this year around the province. The job is not like any other, but I find it interesting and it has certainly given me a much wider understanding of the issues facing the legal system in Northern Ireland, including regulatory issues and statutory issues.'

Barristers: England and Wales

Academic stage

The academic stage of training required to become a barrister is the same as that required to become a solicitor. It is only once a student reaches the vocational stage of training that the qualification routes for solicitors and barristers diverge. Please see the section on qualifying as a solicitor for details on A levels, law degrees, and the GDL. A good academic background is even more important for aspiring barristers than it is for solicitors: it is going to be very difficult to obtain a pupillage (see below) unless you achieve at least a 2.i at degree level.

Vocational stage

Bar Professional Training Course

To become a barrister entitled to practise, the Bar Council requires you to take the one-year (full-time) or two-year (part-time) Bar Professional Training Course (BPTC), previously known as the Bar Vocational Course (BVC). A partial distance learning course is also available. Before registering on the BPTC you will need to be admitted to one of the four Inns of Court: Gray's Inn, Inner Temple, Lincoln's Inn, or Middle Temple (all based in central London). These Inns provide support for barristers and student members, advocacy training and other continuing professional development opportunities, lunching and dining facilities and access to common rooms and gardens. The Inns are also responsible for Calling barristers to the Bar, which is the mechanism by which students become barristers once they have completed the BPTC and pupillage (see below).

The BPTC aims to help you gain the knowledge of procedure and evidence and skills of advocacy, conference skills, drafting, legal research, negotiation and opinion writing to prepare you for the practical stage of training on the job, the one year of pupillage. The BPTC is available at 13 different teaching institutions throughout the country:

- BPP University (Birmingham, Leeds, London, Bristol and Manchester)
- The University of Law (Birmingham, Bristol, Leeds and London)
- Cardiff Law School
- City Law School
- Manchester Metropolitan University
- Nottingham Law School, Nottingham Trent University
- University of the West of England, Bristol
- University of Northumbria, Newcastle.

The BPTC costs between £13,000 and £19,000 depending on the chosen institute.

Applications for the BPTC must be made through the centralised applications system run by the Bar Student Application Service, which has an online application form (www.barsas.com). The system opens for application in the November before the anticipated year of entry and the closing date is usually in the following January, though the exact closing date can be found on the Bar Student Application Service website. An application fee of £58 is payable.

Bar Course Aptitude Test (BCAT)

The Bar Standards Board introduced the Bar Course Aptitude Test (BCAT) which applicants for the BPTC have to pass before their offer of a place on the BPTC can be confirmed. The purpose of the BCAT is to test applicants' critical thinking and reasoning, which are considered to be the core skills required for the BPTC. The idea is to make sure that students starting the BPTC have the necessary skills to pass it.

The test comprises 60 multiple-choice questions that must be completed in 55 minutes. The test is computerised and must be sat at a Pearson VUE centre. The fee for taking the test is £150 if it is taken in UK and EU test centres and £170 for non-EU test centres. For more information on the BCAT, including a practice test so that you can familiarise yourself with the type of questions asked, visit www.bar standardsboard.org.uk/qualifying-as-a-barrister/current-requirements/ bar-professional-training-course/bar-course-aptitude-test.

In 2016, the Bar Standards Board made some modifications to the scoring system. Results on the BCAT are highly reflective of a student's success on the BPTC and, as such, applicants will now be provided with their numerical score as opposed to their pass or fail result, so that they can make an informed decision about pursuing the rigorous and costly programme. In addition, the pass score has increased from 37 to 45 to exclude students who are unlikely to perform well on the BPTC.

Pupillage

Pupillage is the final stage to qualifying as a barrister and is hard work. The first six months of pupillage (known as the 'first six') are non-practising and involve training with a senior barrister (your 'pupil supervisor') at work for six months. During the first six months you will be expected to undertake legal research, draft opinions, and read your pupil supervisor's paperwork.

Once you have completed the first six months, you will spend the second six months (the 'second six') practising and be able to appear in court as an advocate. This is when you start to build your own reputation and have your own cases. Pupils must be paid a minimum salary of £12,000 per annum, plus reasonable travel expenses where applicable.

Those of you eager to become a barrister are in for a tough time. Competition for places is very high. The Bar Standards Board website even includes a Health Warning to warn about the intense competition for pupillages. In 2016, it reported that around 1,400 students enrolled on the bar course, whereas the number of pupillages available in that year was only around 424. To make things even tougher, students are allowed to try to find a pupillage for up to five years after completing the bar course, so in any one year, there could be over 3,000 people applying for pupillages. Some barristers' chambers report having over a hundred applicants for each pupillage placement. Even if you are successful in obtaining a pupillage, there is no guarantee of work after completing it – in every year, there are usually fewer tenancies available at chambers than there are students completing their pupillages, and the opportunities for employed barristers are few and far between. The Bar Standards Board recommends undertaking thorough research to find out if a career at the Bar is really for you, and this includes making a realistic assessment of whether you have the capacity to become a good barrister.

| Students completing BPTC in 2015/2016 | 777 |
| Pupillages available in 2015/2016 | 424 |

Table 4: Competition for barristers' pupillages

Applications for pupillage are made through an online pupillage application system, called 'Pupillage Gateway', which is operated by the Bar Council. The system allows applicants to search and apply for pupillage vacancies. All pupillage providers must advertise all pupillage vacancies on the Gateway. There is a common timetable for the application process, which is typically as follows:

- November: Gateway pupillages are listed for browsing and a practice application form becomes available
- January: submission window opens
- February: submission window closes
- February to April: interview period
- May: offers made.

No charge is made to applicants. For more information and specific dates for the application process for a particular year, visit www.pupillage gateway.com.

Before applying, you should find out as much as possible about your preferred set of chambers. You should study the chambers' website carefully and look at online bar directories. You should also try to attend a pupillage fair. These are held every so often to enable students who wish to pursue a career at the Bar to meet different sets of chambers.

Case study

Emma is a barrister at a large set of chambers, based in London, and specialises in personal injury cases. She took a somewhat convoluted route to the Bar. 'I studied psychology, philosophy and music for A level. I didn't put in nearly enough effort and my grades were not what they should have been, which I suspect hampered my applications for pupillage later on.' After a degree in drama at Loughborough, Emma obtained a Masters in Chinese Law, Politics and Mandarin from the School of Oriental and African Studies (SOAS).

'I had always been told I would be a good lawyer, but I didn't understand what the job involved. I don't have any lawyers in my family and I thought I would have to represent people accused of serious crimes. What I didn't appreciate is that you can be a lawyer without ever doing a criminal case. It wasn't until I was studying for my master's that I started to understand what being a lawyer involved. Initially I wasn't sure whether I wanted to be a solicitor or a barrister but work experience very quickly made things clear for me. My first mini pupillage was a whirlwind of excitement, whereas I kept falling asleep when I did work experience at solicitors' firms! Most people tend to know pretty quickly which role suits them better.'

Having obtained the necessary academic qualification in law by taking the GDL, Emma obtained an Outstanding for the BVC (now called the BPTC). 'The difficult part was getting a pupillage. I worked as a paralegal on very poor pay for one year after Bar school in order to improve the legal experience section on my CV. I ended up giving up paid employment altogether for a month in order to focus on ensuring I had time to take on some Free Representation Unit work that I felt would bolster my CV. Showing that you are dedicated to the legal profession and that you understand what it involves is crucial when it comes to pupillage applications.'

Emma tends to be in court most days, be it for a five-minute application or an all-day trial. On top of that, she has various Advices, Particulars of Claim or Defences to draft. 'The hours vary. Being organised and efficient in your working habits is very important if you want to keep a work/life balance. While I often work in the evenings and weekends, I'm always home for supper, find time for lots of sport and manage to have drinks with friends fairly regularly.'

Emma believes that the skills required to be a barrister vary depending what area of law you specialise in. 'It is very important for all barristers to be well prepared for a case. However, in my line of work cases often change at the last minute or you only get instructed at 6 p.m. the night before a 10 a.m. hearing. A flexible approach and an ability to respond to last minute issues is crucial, as is being able to perform damage limitation when things go wrong. Being polite, pragmatic and generally decent towards judges, court staff and other barristers also goes a long way.'

Funding your qualification

The average cost of completing the vocational stage of training is estimated at over £20,000 if living expenses are taken into account. The fees for the BPTC for 2016/2017 were between £13,250 and £19,070 for the year. Only a limited number of awards, grants and scholarships are available for the vocational stage of Bar training. The Inns of Court offer a range of scholarships and some chambers give awards towards the BPTC. However, the majority of students have to depend on bank loans or other forms of support. Please refer to the individual chambers' websites or the Bar Council website for further details.

Advocates: Scotland

The academic and vocational stages are the same as qualifying as a solicitor in Scotland (see the section on qualifying as a solicitor in Scotland on page 57). The intending advocate in Scotland needs to take a law degree followed by the postgraduate Diploma in Professional Legal Practice plus a minimum of 21 months' training in a Scottish solicitor's office.

This is followed by nine months' further unpaid practical training called 'devilling', or work-shadowing. Initially, this involves a Foundation course where the pupils' oral and written advocacy skills are developed through intensive workshops and seminars. There are further compulsory skills courses that must be completed. Pupils will also work for an experienced advocate who has been practising for more than seven years (a 'devilmaster'), to gain experience of civil practice and the criminal courts. Passing the Diploma in Professional Legal Practice culminates in the completion of the Faculty of Advocates' written examinations. The Faculty does not charge for the training and scholarships are available to support with living costs.

Please visit the Faculty of Advocates website for more information: www.advocates.org.uk/about-advocates/becoming-an-advocate/information-for-students.

Barristers: Northern Ireland

Details on how to qualify as a barrister in Northern Ireland are available on the website of the Bar of Northern Ireland (www.barofni.com/page/becoming-a-barrister). Very briefly, the academic stage is the same as for qualifying as a solicitor; students must have completed a recognised law degree (see the section on qualifying as a solicitor in Northern Ireland on page 60).

For the vocational stage of training, students must complete the one year full-time Bar Postgraduate Diploma in Professional Legal Studies at the Institute of Professional Legal Studies, Queen's University, Belfast (the IPLS).

After graduating from the Institute when they have passed the Bar course, students are called to the Bar of Northern Ireland. Bar trainees must then undertake a pupillage with a master for a period of 12 months.

Case study

David is a barrister who works in Northern Ireland. He initially qualified as a medical doctor, but transferred to the profession later.

'I initially qualified as a medical doctor in 1990 having studied science at A level. I enjoyed this work but realised that it was not what I wanted to do long term and that I had perhaps taken a wrong direction in my final years at school when I had also thought about law. I spoke to a very senior consultant who had a strong family connection to law and he advised me to spend a few years in medicine and take some postgraduate medical qualifications. I took his advice and specialised in emergency medicine, gaining MRP and FRCS.

'It was at this stage that I decided to convert to law and undertook the two-year law degree at Queen's University, Belfast. I was then successful in the admissions exam to the Institute and completed a year of full-time study before being called to the Northern Ireland Bar in 1999. I have since been called to the Bars of England and Ireland. I am a member of the Bar Library Belfast and 12KBW London.

'I now undertake a wide range of legal work, including commercial, property, clinical negligence, construction, planning and more. I have been a Pupil Master to five pupil barristers and I regularly deliver CPD talks.'

---

5 | Getting work experience

Getting work experience is crucial in terms of helping you secure a training contract or pupillage in today's extremely competitive climate. It is not enough to be purely a brilliant academic. The more relevant experience you have, the better the chance of succeeding.

You can apply for work experience at any stage in the qualification process, whether it be during A levels, during a law (or other) degree, or even at a later stage if you are having trouble obtaining a training contract or pupillage. There are many types of vacation schemes run by the larger firms of solicitors, and chambers also offer mini pupillages; these are invaluable ways of gaining experience and getting a foot in the door. You will be much more attractive to potential employers if you can show that you have relevant work experience. Most of these work experience schemes are only available to undergraduates.

However, having some work experience is also very useful in applying to university for a law degree. You are less likely to be able to find a place on a formal work experience programme while you are still at school, but you should still look for some sort of experience just to get you into a legal environment and see what lawyers actually do. This will support your application for a law degree and help you write the personal statement on your UCAS form (see Chapter 7, pages 96–105).

What have you got to gain from work experience?

When considering a career in any field, work experience is an excellent way of gaining an invaluable insight into the profession. Work placements within a legal setting will enable you to see whether a career in law is for you. You should endeavour to organise placements, either independently or through your school, into the specific field of law in which you are interested. If you are unsure, try and obtain experience in various areas to enhance your knowledge of the different areas within the legal field. Work experience would be beneficial for a number of reasons, including the following.

- It will give you a real insight into the profession. You will be able to observe the day-to-day duties of legal professionals and identify the skills that their roles command. It will also give you an excellent opportunity to weigh up the pros and cons of becoming a lawyer. This can be further explored by discussing the profession with the individuals that you are working with, as they will be able to give you honest answers to your questions. Finally, you will be able to see whether being a barrister or a solicitor is for you, and if it is the latter, the type of law firm in which you would prefer to work.

- By observing legal professionals in practice and reflecting on their duties, you will be much more informed when discussing your interests and aptitude in your personal statement when applying for a law degree at university, and in your applications for legal jobs. Undertaking these placements will demonstrate your commitment to a career in law, and prove that you have given it some real thought.
- Working with legal professionals will allow you to build those all-important contacts that will be beneficial in an extremely competitive environment. Providing that you are able to demonstrate your enthusiasm and willingness to learn, you should be able to secure some strong references, as well as the possibility of acquiring further placements at a later stage.
- By developing your knowledge of what a particular role entails and getting a feel for the pace and demands of the job, work experience will help you to make the transition into full-time work once you have completed the academic component of qualification.

However, it is not that easy getting legal work experience, and can in itself be a competitive process. Most universities and employers recognise this and do not stipulate that work experience is essential, although it is preferred and you should put some considerable effort into obtaining some. This will allow you to reflect on the skill set commanded and demonstrate that you are conscious of the skills that need to be developed. If you cannot get experience in a firm of solicitors or chambers, any work experience that demonstrates use of the skills they are interested in will be valuable. Skills such as communication, determination and business awareness can all be developed in many other sectors of business and commerce. Even just showing that you can get up every day and present yourself for work at 9 o'clock in the morning is of some use.

There are also other ways of gaining relevant legal experience while you are at school or university, for example, participating in a debating society or in mooting or mock trials will help hone your advocacy skills. Some university students hoping to enter the legal profession volunteer at their university law centre or law clinic.

Admissions tutors recognise the fact that obtaining work experience in a legal environment can be extremely difficult, so it is generally not viewed as a requirement for acceptance onto an undergraduate course. Generally, universities state that if you are able to undertake work experience, it will undoubtedly benefit your understanding of what the role entails and therefore support your application. However, being unable to do so will not put applicants at a disadvantage. In essence, any way in which you can demonstrate that you have made the effort to develop your understanding of what a career in law involves will be viewed as being beneficial. This could be demonstrated through wider reading, extra-curricular activities and visits to law courts, for example. Academic attainment is the main reason behind offers being made, though if an offer is narrowly missed, a strong overall application based on a competent knowledge of what the course and career entails could allow for some leniency on results day.

Similarly, employers understand that securing mini pupillages or placements on vacation schemes is tough owing to the extremely competitive climate. While it is inevitable that the knowledge and skills obtained on these placements will be invaluable in your development as a lawyer, the same skills can be developed elsewhere, such as mooting experience, voluntary work and alternative work experience placements. Mini pupillages and vacation schemes are designed to be enjoyable and useful, but they are not a pre-requisite for securing a pupillage or a training contract.

If you look through the case studies contained in this book, it is noticeable that all the young lawyers did a variety of work experience while at school and university, and they all think it played an important part in landing them a job at the end of their studies.

Things to consider during work experience

Work experience placements provide you with excellent opportunities to cultivate knowledge of the field and an understanding of the career. As a result, it is crucial that you are aware of what is going on around you so that you can develop your insight.

Making a good impression

In general, you should aim to maintain a high level of professionalism throughout the duration of your placement. Remember, the legal professionals that you work with at this point could play a crucial role in the development of your career at a later stage. With this in mind, always try to adopt the following attitudes.

- **Maintain a formal position:** dress smartly and present yourself appropriately. If you are unsure of how to dress, it is always better to wear more formal attire.
- **Be polite:** offer to help with routine tasks where sensible and aim to show your interest by asking questions. In general, people will be quite flattered when you show an interest in their role and how they reached that point in their career, so don't be afraid to demonstrate your curiosity! If you show that you are friendly and reliable, there is a greater chance of you acquiring more opportunities.

- **Be organised:** make sure that you are on time and plan your commute accordingly. Punctuality makes a lasting impression! You should also make sure that you take anything with you that might be required, such as a pen, a notebook and any formal documentation that may have been requested, such as proof of identification. Similarly, make sure that you organise your time effectively so that you can complete set tasks, and note down the times of meetings or hearings that you have been invited to attend.
- **Be enthusiastic:** demonstrate your competence by completing all tasks that you are set, and don't shy away from responsibility. No one is expecting you to get everything right – work experience is a learning curve, so get stuck in! If you think you have something valuable to say, raise it. Regardless of whether your suggestion is taken up, it will give employers a chance to see that you are really interested.

Doing all of these things will get you on the right track for making the most of your work experience placement. It is also worth considering the following aspects.

The qualities possessed by lawyers

Depending on whether a lawyer is practising as a barrister or a solicitor, they will need to possess and consistently exhibit a range of skills that allow them to carry out their roles successfully. During your placement, it is important to keep a keen eye on the characteristics that the lawyer demonstrates when carrying out their everyday duties. Being able to reflect on these qualities will be an important part of your qualification process; in written applications it will show your knowledge about the skills required to excel in the field, and provide useful aspects to discuss at interview. It will also allow you to identify traits that you need to develop yourself.

Day-to-day tasks

A work experience placement will give you a really thorough insight into a typical day for a solicitor or a barrister. Though it can be argued that there is no 'typical day' and tasks can be quite varied, it should give you a strong indication of what is expected. From this, you should be able to determine whether a career as a solicitor or a barrister is for you.

Solicitors tend to work with clients more closely, typically as part of a larger team. As such, solicitors must hone their communication skills to effectively convey legal positions in layman's terms. This contrasts heavily with the independent work of a barrister, who must then present cases in court following instruction from a client or solicitor. Therefore, the daily tasks for each job could differ significantly, and work experience should allow you to see which elements appeal to you and which do not.

The roles of other legal professionals

Through your time in a legal practice, it is important to consider the roles of staff other than solicitors or barristers. For example, legal secretaries, paralegals and legal executives will all work alongside and for solicitors, and it is essential to acquire an understanding of how these individuals work together to form a functional team. Make sure that you take the time to speak to as many people in different roles as possible, showing an interest in the specific tasks that they undertake.

Working as a lawyer

There is no denying that qualifying as a lawyer is tough, with high demands and long hours. It is for this reason that it is so important that you ask questions about these aspects: find out which areas of the job lawyers find rewarding, and which areas they dislike.

Keeping a work experience diary

Your work experience will likely be fundamental when looking to develop your career. With this in mind, it is worth you making notes of any interesting observations so that you have a full record to review in preparation for university applications, job applications and interviews.

It is advisable to lay out a formal diary in which you list your daily activities, noting down any key observations regarding specific tasks that were undertaken by lawyers and the skills that they used to conduct them effectively. Keeping a notebook with you will also allow you to jot down any questions that you may have, as well as the answers given to those questions.

Where to apply for work experience

Law firms' vacation schemes for aspiring solicitors

The big corporate law firms offer a range of different vacation schemes, and if you are at all interested in this type of law, you should apply for some of these while studying law at undergraduate level. If you are interested in commercial law, but do not necessarily want to train at one of the biggest firms, it is still useful to have done one of these vacation schemes as it will impress any smaller commercial firm that you may apply to for a training contract by showing that you have done your research into working as a commercial solicitor. Even if you are not sure what type of law you are really interested in (or, indeed, whether you would like to become a solicitor or barrister) it is worth applying for some of these schemes as it may help you make up your mind.

There are different sorts of schemes depending on what stage of your education you are at and whether or not you are studying law at university. Many firms offer shorter 'taster' schemes for first year undergraduates, followed by slightly longer schemes (of two, three or four weeks) for students in their penultimate year of university. The same schemes may be open to those taking a non-law degree, or different schemes may be available. Most take place during the summer, but some are available during other university holiday periods. To research these vacation schemes, you need to look at the websites of all the big law firms (some of which are listed in Chapter 3). There are often strict application timetables that require you to apply up to a year in advance (so, for example, in the first term of the academic year for a placement the following summer).

Generally, vacation schemes pay a small amount of money to cover your expenses while you are there. Many of these big firms link their vacation schemes to their training contracts. You may not necessarily have to do a vacation scheme to be offered a training contract, but it will certainly help, and some firms use vacation schemes as a way of finding suitable candidates to offer training contracts to. Some firms recruit trainees almost exclusively from their vacation schemes. They will also give you a genuine insight into the culture of the different firms and help you decide where you would like to work. One junior solicitor commented that she only applied to firms that she had done a vacation scheme with as she knew much more about what they were like and whether she would enjoy working there.

Mini pupillages at chambers

Similarly, many barristers' chambers offer mini pupillages, which allow you to shadow a practising barrister for up to two weeks to find out what working as a barrister is really like. If you think that there is any possibility that you might like to become a barrister, then it is crucial to try hard to undertake a mini pupillage. You can search online for barristers' chambers that offer mini pupillages and there are also online search tools available, such as at www.lawcareers.net.

'Informal' placements

Work experience can also take place on less of a formal basis than a vacation scheme or mini pupillage through shadowing court officers or a barristers' clerk. Such work experience would be invaluable for a university application.

As vacation schemes are incredibly competitive and only offered by a small subset of practices, you can take a speculative approach to applying by contacting law firms directly. This could involve a phone call, email or face-to-face discussion initially, but is usually followed up by sending in a CV and covering letter for consideration. An excellent time to procure such placements would be during summer and Easter breaks.

Both the Law Society and the Legal 500 list UK law firms with contact details and provide a useful source of information when making speculative applications.

In the same way, you can also approach sets of chambers that do not offer formal mini pupillage schemes. The Chambers and Partners directory provide the names and addresses of UK chambers.

Voluntary work

Some legal work can be undertaken on a voluntary basis and, for several reasons, conducting such work would prove to be invaluable in terms of developing the necessary skills to succeed in the field of law.

Perhaps the most useful voluntary work that can be undertaken to enhance your legal skills is voluntary work at a law clinic, which is accessible to undergraduate students. A variety of roles can be undertaken, and all of these will allow you to witness first-hand the range of queries that arise and the manner in which they are dealt.

The Citizens Advice Bureau and the Free Representation Unit also provide volunteer opportunities with a legal basis, giving you the opportunity to gain experience in dealing with several legal issues such as housing and welfare law. It will also allow you to develop your understanding of how to appropriately advise clients.

However, voluntary work does not necessarily have to have a legal basis for it to be useful. Volunteer work in any field presents a wide range of opportunities to engage with people from different backgrounds and age groups, and gain new or develop existing skills as well as confidence. Maintaining a long-term voluntary position demonstrates an individual's commitment to helping society and developing their skills in communication. It will also give you the chance to enhance your understanding of the wider world.

As most charitable organisations are enthusiastic about recruiting volunteers, securing a placement should not be too difficult. Examples of areas that could be considered include:

- **charity work:** typically involves working in a charity shop or supporting the fundraising efforts of a charitable organisation
- **care work:** provides the opportunity to develop your communication skills when working with vulnerable people
- **humanitarian work:** will improve your understanding of wider international issues, potentially presenting you with the opportunity to overcome obstacles in communication such as language barriers
- **educational work:** supporting students in schools or voluntary teaching roles, e.g. teaching English to refugees.

Information on voluntary positions can be found on a number of websites, including:

- Do-It (https://do-it.org)
- Volunteering Matters (https://volunteeringmatters.org.uk)
- NCVO (www.ncvo.org.uk/ncvo-volunteering/i-want-to-volunteer)
- Volunteer Scotland (www.volunteerscotland.net)
- Volunteer Wales (www.volunteering-wales.net).

Other potential sources of useful experience

Outside of work experience and voluntary placements, additional valuable experience could be obtained elsewhere.

- Internships within the legal sector, which typically last several months and take place during the summer holidays.
- Joining an Inn provides opportunities in mentorship, marshalling with a judge and in-house societies for aspiring barristers.
- Extra-curricular activities, such as involvement in law societies at university, participating in debating societies and mooting competitions. Similarly, joining finance-related societies could prove to be beneficial if you are considering a career in the commercial sector.
- Courts allow the public to observe lawyers in action, making this an easy way to observe court activity.

Looking through the case studies (and example personal statements) contained in this book will also give you some ideas.

Try as many ways of getting work experience as you can think of and be creative in the process. Here are a few suggestions.

- Ask your teachers at school/college if they have any contacts in the legal profession.
- Use your careers service and speak to your careers officer.
- Talk to your family and friends and ask them if they can suggest anyone to contact.
- Make sure everyone you know is aware you are looking for work experience.
- You can also approach sets of chambers that do not offer formal mini pupillage schemes. The Chambers and Partners directory will also give you names and addresses of chambers.

While you are trying to get work experience, you should make sure that you keep up to date with current affairs relating to the legal world and the legal profession by reading a quality broadsheet newspaper and looking at specialist journals such as *The Law Society Gazette* and *The Lawyer*, which should both be available from large public libraries and are also online (see Chapter 12, page 141 for details).

You should ask to go in for one or two weeks' work experience during the holidays or even just ask for one day's work-shadowing to get an insight into what the working environment is like. Anything that anyone is prepared to give you will be useful. Whichever route you take will almost certainly be unpaid unless you have specific skills to offer, such as good office and keyboard skills. If you can touch-type, you could try to get some paid work with a firm of solicitors during the summer or register with an employment agency.

How to apply

CV

Many formal vacation schemes and mini pupillages will require you to apply online using an application form. For anything else, you will probably need to put together a CV to support your application. This is a summary of what you have done in your life to date. If you have hardly any work experience then one page on good-quality A4 paper will be sufficient. If you are a mature student with a lot of jobs behind you there is sometimes a case for going on to a second page. So what should go into your CV? Here are the main headings:

- name
- contact details
- education and qualifications
- previous work experience.

There is no standard CV but there is a sample opposite. Make sure to include the following points. You should ensure that you don't leave any gaps and account for all your time. Also, if something such as illness prevented you from reaching your potential in your exams, point this out in the covering letter (see below). Lawyers have excellent attention to detail, so make sure your spelling and grammar are perfect!

Education

Start with your present school, college or university and work back to the beginning of secondary school. No primary schools please! List the qualifications with grades you already have and the ones you intend to sit.

Work experience

Start with the most recent. Don't worry if you've only had a Saturday job at the local shop or a paper round. Put it all down and focus on drawing out any relevant skills that you have gained from it. Employers like to see that you are able to carefully consider your experiences.

Skills

List those such as computer skills, software packages used, languages and driving licence.

A sample CV

PERSONAL DETAILS
Mike Davies
81 Bridgewater Drive
Wolverhampton WV14 9RS
01234 567890
mikedavies@btinternet.com

EDUCATION & QUALIFICATIONS
2010–present: Elmfield High School and Sixth Form,
Wolverhampton
Currently undertaking three A levels: Law, History and English
language and literature
9 GCSEs (obtained in August 2015): English language (A), English
literature (A), Maths (A), Geography (A), German (A), Latin (A),
Physical Education (B), Science (B), Additional Science (C)

WORK EXPERIENCE
Wilkins bakery, July 2015–present: Part-time customer assistant.
I prepare and cook food, serve customers and handle cash in a
particularly busy store.
Elmfield High School, September 2014–present: Volunteer.
I support international students with the development of their
English language skills.
James & Co. Accountants, July 2014–August 2014: One month
work experience placement.
I was responsible for answering telephone calls and conducting
general clerical work.

SKILLS
Computing: competent in use of Word, Excel and PowerPoint.

POSITIONS OF RESPONSIBILITY
Prefect at Elmfield High School: responsible for setting a good
example to younger students, and maintaining and promoting
excellent behaviour

INTERESTS
Playing rugby (at county level), reading classical literature and
learning Spanish through self-teaching.

REFERENCES

Mr A Jones	Mrs B Greene
Personal Tutor	James & Co. Accountants
Elmfield High School	26 Castle Street
Wolverhampton	Wolverhampton
ajones@elmfield.ac.uk	bgreene@jamesandco.co.uk

Interests and positions of responsibility

What do you like to do in your spare time? If you are or have been captain of a sports team, been a committee member or even head boy or head girl at school, put it all down.

Referees

Usually two: an academic referee such as a teacher or head of your school plus someone who knows you well personally, who is not a relative, such as someone for whom you have worked.

Covering letter

Every CV or application form should always be accompanied by a covering letter. The letter is important because it is usually the first thing a potential employer reads.

Here are some tips.

- The letter should be on the same A4 plain paper as your CV and should look like a professional document. It should be no longer than one side of A4.
- Employers accept typed letters, unless they specifically request one to be handwritten.
- Find out the name of the person to whom you should send your letter and CV. It makes a great difference to the reader if you can personalise your application. If you start the letter 'Dear Mr Brown', remember you should finish it 'Yours sincerely'.
- The first paragraph should tell the reader why you are contacting them and what stage of your education you are at.
- The second paragraph should give them some brief information to make them interested in you, e.g. highlighting your interest in law, along with some specific IT skills.
- Thirdly, you should explain why you are applying to them, for example interest in their line of work, desire to experience work in a small/large firm/set, etc. Mention anything you already know about the firm/chambers and make sure that it is correct. Look carefully at their website and make sure you know what area of the law they practise in!
- Check very carefully for spelling and grammatical mistakes.

A sample covering letter is shown below.

Dear Mr Cooper,

I am currently in my first year of my A level study at Elmfield High School and intend to study law at undergraduate level at university. To strengthen my application, I am interested in securing a work experience placement, and wondered whether SPM LLP would have any opportunities available.

I am extremely interested in the field of family law, and can see from your website that SPM LLP has an outstanding reputation for dealing with family law and that your work is recognised both nationally and internationally.

I am currently undertaking the Extended Project Qualification in law and the independent research that I have conducted for this that has drawn me into this particular area. I have strong IT and typing skills, as well as good communication skills that I have developed by voluntarily teaching English to international students.

Please do not hesitate to contact me if you require any further information or would like me to come to your office to meet you in person.

Yours sincerely,

Mike Davies

Case study

Alesha is currently in her third year of a law degree at the University of Warwick.

'Prior to starting my law degree, I had not obtained any legal work experience as it is difficult to obtain. However, I had always been interested in law as an academic subject and learning about its operation in society. Attending the Crown Court and sitting in on cases allowed me to explore my interest and helped me to decide that it was a career that I could really see myself following in the future. I also attended lectures given by barristers and scholars of law. While providing a great opportunity to learn more about my chosen field, this was also a really good way to network and speak to legal professionals, which allowed me to learn about the way that law is practised and implemented.

'I studied humanities-based subjects at A level, including English literature, politics, history and classics. These provided a really good foundation for developing my essay writing skills and prepared me for the vast amount of reading required for studying law at undergraduate level! Getting the A level grades required is by far the most important aspect of your application, especially when aiming to secure a place at a top university, and this will also impact your employability later in life. I would advise getting involved with extra-curricular activities such as debating, as this will help to make your application stand out and provide examples where you can demonstrate your advocacy skills.

'When trying to identify the right university for you, it is important to look at the modules taught in each of the years and its assessment methods. At Warwick, I have really enjoyed learning about how law relates directly to society as a whole. Global intellectual property law and international law have been the modules that I have found the most interesting and are the fields that I am considering as a career. It is also well worth investigating the department's links to solicitors' firms and chambers, as these will be crucial in helping you secure placements and experience in the future.

'Most universities will provide law-specific societies and I would encourage getting involved as much as possible, as applying for graduate positions is extremely competitive so you will need to stand out! I have been involved in a number of activities, including:

- participating in first year CMS mooting competition
- participating in Warwick witness examination competition
- attending a "Day in the City" event which involved visiting Chambers in London and the Royal Courts of Justice
- getting involved with societies and becoming Vice President of the Warwick Bar Society for aspiring barristers (where I was also able to develop important skills in organising the Law Ball)
- an internship at the Houses of Parliament
- participating in an international venture – Warwick Finance Societies in Dubai
- attending insight days at Dubai Islamic Bank, PwC, The Boston Consulting Group, AL Tamimi & Company, Freshfields Bruckhaus Deringer, Linklaters, Francis Taylor Building and Quadrant Chambers
- mini pupillages at St Ives Chambers and 2 Bedford Row
- being Campus Representative for The University of Law.

'Undertaking all of these additional elements has been time consuming, and some of them have been difficult to secure, but they have been invaluable in allowing me to learn new skills, gain hands-on experience that I can use to demonstrate those skills and identify what exactly I want to pursue as a career.

'I hope to become a barrister following graduation. At the moment, I am applying for the BPTC and trying to secure funding through an Inns of Court Scholarship. I will then undertake a pupillage as a training year before eventually being called to the Bar.'

6 | Choosing your university law course

This chapter focuses on how to go about choosing a law degree. The aim is to produce a shortlist of degree courses you are interested in and from that to choose the top five courses to put down in your UCAS application.

As previous chapters have made clear, you do not need a law degree to enter the legal profession. Equally, a law degree can be an excellent springboard into a wide range of other careers. Employers are generally impressed by a good-calibre law graduate, since law is known to be a challenging discipline requiring skills such as research, analysis, application, clarity, advocacy and effective written communication. These are relevant in many other careers as well as those in the legal professions.

If you do not wish to read law at university, most of the advice in this chapter will still be relevant to choosing your degree course, but for more general advice on choosing degree courses, please refer to some of the guides mentioned in Chapter 12.

Things to consider

The basic criteria for choosing your degree course are:

- the type of law course you are interested in
- your academic ability
- where you want to study.

Most of the information you need to know about universities and the courses available at them is available online either through:

- UCAS (www.ucas.com)
- universities' own websites. Most universities have their prospectuses available to download online (although you can request a paper copy to be sent through the post if you prefer) and there should also be information on who to contact if you have a specific question.
- university comparison guides and league tables such as the Complete University Guide (www.thecompleteuniversityguide.co. uk) and the Guardian University Guide (www.theguardian.com/

education/ng-interactive/2017/may/16/university-league-tables-2018). There are also books providing similar information, such as *The Times and Sunday Times Good University Guide*. Make sure you use the most up-to-date edition.

Going to university is an investment, particularly with the rise in tuition fees in recent years, so the choice of what to study and where to apply to must be given careful thought. You will also spend three years of your life there, so you will want to make sure that you will be somewhere you will enjoy living. There are many institutions offering law courses and you will need to look at ways of narrowing down your options.

Types of law degree

Many law degree courses are offered by many different institutions across the country and the choice may at first appear daunting. However, the range of options can quickly be narrowed down once you know what you are looking for. The important thing is to choose the right course for you. The key points to consider are:

- if you intend to qualify as a solicitor or a barrister in the future, the degree must be a qualifying law degree (QLD) if you wish to go straight onto the LPC afterwards
- whether you should choose an LLB or a BA (and whether it matters)
- should you choose a single or joint honours degree?

Qualifying law degrees

Qualifying law degrees are recognised by the Law Society and the Bar Council, and only QLDs allow students to progress directly to the vocational stage of training. This means that you do not need to spend an extra year taking the GDL after you graduate. A list of the institutions that offer QLDs and lists of the different courses they offer can be found at www.sra.org.uk/students/courses/qualifying-law-degree-providers.page. All qualifying law degrees will cover the following seven core subjects (sometimes referred to as the seven foundations of legal knowledge):

1. contract
2. tort (often referred to, with contract, as obligations)
3. criminal law
4. public law, including constitutional law, administrative law and human rights law
5. property law (or land law)
6. equity and the law of trusts
7. law of the European Union.

The Glossary contains an explanation of these terms. You will also learn about legal research techniques and the English (or Scottish or Northern Irish) legal system.

As is explained in Chapter 4, for a law degree to constitute a QLD, the Law Society requires you to study legal subjects for at least two-thirds of the time (for a three-year degree course). At least half of a normal three-year degree course must be spent on the foundation subjects listed above. This means that there will be a lot of similarities between QLDs as they all spend half the time, at least, on the above subjects. However, the rest of the course content, and the range of optional subjects available, will vary considerably. The style of teaching and the approach taken to studying law will also vary (see below for more information on different approaches to studying law).

LLB or BA?

Some law degrees are classified as LLBs, whereas others are BAs. As a broad generalisation, LLB degrees will involve spending all of your time studying law, whereas a BA or BSc degree may involve spending some time studying non-law modules. However, so long as the degree is a QLD, all of the core legal subjects will still be covered, and whether you end up with an LLB or BA will not affect your ability to pursue a legal (or any other) career. For historical reasons, the universities of Oxford and Cambridge do not award LLBs at all and their law degrees are BAs. If you are interested in studying non-law modules as part of your law degree (for example, foreign languages), then the increased breadth may well be interesting and valuable for you and also welcomed by future employers.

Single or joint honours?

Law can be taken on its own (a single honours degree) or mixed with one or more other subjects (a joint honours degree).

A single honours degree will allow you to focus on studying law, although some courses will also permit you to take individual modules from other subject areas, even from completely different disciplines. As well as the core subjects, you will also be able to choose optional subjects (particularly in second and later years). Some institutions can offer only a limited selection of options, while others provide a much greater variety. If there is a particular area of law you are interested in, for example intellectual property law, then you may want to apply to a university that offers this as an option.

A joint honours degree will allow you to divide your time between law and one or more other disciplines. Usually, where two subjects in a degree title are joined by the word 'and', this indicates that the course will involve a 50/50 split between the two subjects, whereas the word 'with' suggest a two-thirds/one-third split. However, this is a broad generalisation and you should always check the details of any particular course on the university's website. A joint honours degree course must satisfy the Law Society's requirements if it is to qualify as a QLD (see above), so it is likely that joint honours degrees that are QLDs involve spending more than half the time studying law. A popular combination is to study law with a European language, although you should note that these courses often specify that candidates must have an A level or at the very least a GCSE in the relevant language.

It is important to check that any joint honours degrees in particular are QLDs (see above) if you want to go on to be a solicitor or barrister and want to make sure that your degree will satisfy the academic stage of training so that you do not need to spend an additional year taking the GDL.

Approaches to teaching law

It is interesting to note by way of background that there are broadly three different approaches to teaching law, but you should not base your selection on this criterion since few institutions adhere to one kind. Most places are likely to opt for a mixture (sometimes even within an individual unit, especially if it is taught by several different tutors). However, the emphasis of different law schools may be different. The approaches are as follows.

- *Pure academic approach.* This approach focuses on the core legal subjects and doesn't look much beyond statutes and law reports for its sources of law. It provides a thorough grounding in the relevant legal system and its laws.
- *Contextual approach.* Law can also be examined in context; that is to say, law, its role and its effectiveness are looked at in relation to society (past and present), politics and the economy. This approach may include elements of critical legal theory. Students are expected to analyse the problems (for example, loopholes, contradictions, injustices and so on) within the law. This can make for some heated and controversial seminars.
- *Vocational approach.* This stresses professional training and skills such as negotiating, interviewing, counselling, drafting, research, analysis, clear expression and the ability to read through vast amounts of material, sift out the legally relevant points and present a logical argument. These skills are mainly covered during the vocational stage of training to become a solicitor or barrister, but may also be looked at in a law degree. Extra-curricular activities such as mooting (a mock courtroom trial), debating and law clinics, in which students get the opportunity to help out with a real-life case from start to finish, also help develop these skills at university.

Academic requirements

Entry requirements for law degrees vary greatly, both in terms of the standard that they expect students to have achieved and also in how they are expressed. You will need to research which degrees at which universities your likely A levels, Scottish Highers, IB or BTEC qualifications will enable you to access. It is important to be realistic about the grades you are likely to achieve: don't be too pessimistic, but don't kid yourself about your 'as yet undiscovered' genius. Talk to your teachers for an accurate picture of your predicted results. You can then target your universities accordingly. Don't forget that you need to select one or two universities with lower grade requirements than your predictions as 'insurance' choices.

Most of the top universities offering QLDs require applicants to have three A levels (or their equivalent) and the grade requirements have become even more challenging since the introduction of the A* grade. The most selective universities, such as Cambridge, now regularly include the A* grade in their offers. Information on the entry requirements for law degrees at different universities is available through UCAS or the websites of the universities themselves.

Less academically selective universities often express their entry requirements as a target number of UCAS points using the UCAS Tariff system. This system is used to allocate points to the different qualifications taken by students before they access higher education. It therefore allows students with different types of qualifications to access undergraduate degree courses, and also allows the universities to compare applicants with different qualifications. The UCAS Tariff system was updated for entry in September 2017 to accommodate reforms to qualifications such as A levels. The purpose of the new system is to accommodate the reforms to qualifications currently being introduced (such as the new A levels) and also to enable more vocational qualifications and more international qualifications to earn points, thereby supporting political demands for widening participation. The new UCAS Tariff tables for the different qualifications are available on the UCAS website (www.ucas.com).

Your A level subject choices may also have a bearing on which universities you can realistically expect to receive an offer from. Few courses specify subjects they want you to have studied (with the exception of most language joint degrees), although qualifications in traditional academic subjects are preferred at the more selective universities and are welcomed everywhere. Some universities won't accept A levels such as general studies or critical thinking, and possibly even the less academic ones such as art. No institutions require A level Law from potential students. See Chapter 4, pages 42–45 for more information on A level subject choices. You should always check carefully on the websites of all the universities that you are interested in to confirm their specific requirements.

If your predicted A level results (or chosen A level subjects) effectively prevent you from taking a law degree, then it's time for a rethink. If you wanted to take a law degree with a view to entering the profession, then you could opt for the non-law degree entry route instead. Most employers stress that a large number of trainee solicitors and pupil barristers have a non-law degree. Remember that if you read a subject other than law, you will have to complete the GDL before going on to the LPC or BPTC. The disadvantage is that the route might be longer and therefore more expensive (if sponsorship cannot be found).

Choosing a university

Once you have made a realistic assessment of your likely A level grades (or other qualifications) you can think about choosing specific institutions. Remember, university life isn't going to be solely about academic study. It is truly a growing experience – educationally, socially and culturally – and besides, three or four years can really drag if you're not happy outside the lecture theatre. Here is an assortment of factors which might help you to choose where you would like to study. Some of these will be more important to you than others, so you should use the paragraphs below to think carefully about the things that matter most to you.

Warning: different legal systems

If you're hoping to practise law, then you must be sure where you intend to work within the UK (i.e. England or Wales, Scotland or Northern Ireland). Since the legal systems differ throughout the UK, you must qualify in the part of the UK you intend to practise in in the future. If you did subsequently decide to move, then it would usually be possible to convert qualifications from a different country (e.g. if you qualified in England but want to practise in Scotland). More information can be found by visiting the websites of the Law Societies and Bar Councils for each country, mentioned in Chapter 3. More detail on the differences between the professions in each of the UK countries can be found in Chapters 2 and 3.

Open days

If you get the opportunity, attend the open days for the universities where you are interested in studying. Visit the law departments and talk to former or current students and course lecturers and tutors. Doing so should give you an idea of what life on campus at that particular university is like, and this will allow you to determine whether you would enjoy your time there. If you cannot attend any open days, there are often campus tours available, or you can make an independent visit. Try to go on a taster course for law at any university if possible. This does not need to be a university to which you are actually thinking of applying – even if it is not, it will still give you an idea of what to look for in universities in general and will also give you something to mention in your personal statement (see Chapter 7, pages 96–105).

Types of university or college

There are a number of ways of categorising universities and higher education colleges, but there are two broad categorisations by which these institutions are often sorted:

Old or new?

Almost all law degrees are taught by universities and these can be categorised as 'old' or 'new'. A few other colleges of higher education also offer law degrees:

1. 'Old' universities. Traditionally the more academic universities with higher admission requirements, the old universities are well established, with good libraries and research facilities. They are well respected by employers and provide an academically rigorous training.
2. 'New' universities. Pre-1992, most of these were polytechnics or institutes of higher education and these generally still hold true to the original polytechnic doctrine of vocational courses and strong ties with industry, typically through placements and work experience. Their approach to teaching law may generally be slightly more vocational in nature. They can still be looked down upon by some employers because of their generally lower academic entry requirements, but many of the new universities have a good name for flexible admissions and learning and modern approaches to their degree teaching. There are also some private universities, such as BPP University, the University of Law and Buckingham University. These universities can offer even greater flexibility in the way your degree course is structured. Some private universities now offer the chance to take a degree that would normally take three years in only two years of full-time study, which can be really helpful if you want to qualify as quickly as possible, and possibly of particular interest to mature or overseas students. You will simply forgo the long holidays usually associated with university degree courses. Private universities tend to be more vocational in their approach. They receive no state funding, so are not subject to the Government's cap on tuition fees, but may not necessarily be more expensive, especially if you choose the two-year degree option. Some institutions offer part-time degree courses.

3. Colleges of higher education. Usually these are specialist institutions and therefore provide good facilities in their chosen fields, despite their size. They are sometimes affiliated to universities, which means the college buys the right to teach the degree, which the university will award, provided that the course meets the standards set by the university.
4. The Open University, which is a very well-established provider of part-time distance-learning degree courses, offers an LLB degree that is a qualifying law degree.

City or campus?

Universities are also often divided into campus or city universities. So, when looking at which university to choose you need to consider whether you would prefer to live on a university campus, surrounded by your fellow students and the university's facilities, or whether you would prefer to be more integrated into town or city life. The choice is slightly more sophisticated than this broad division, since many universities offer something of a mix between these two extremes. For example, there are campuses in the middle of, or right on the edge of, cities or towns. Other campuses are practically surrounded by open fields and the nearest town or city is a bus ride away. Some city universities are largely contained in one area, whereas others are spread throughout the city.

The town or city where the university is based, particularly its size, can also have a big effect on the 'feel' of the place. So, for example, some city universities have a largely separate university area, but are close to the centre of a large city (for example, Leeds). Others are more inte- grated into the city (such as Sheffield). Some have a largely self-contained campus, but are still in a big city (such as Nottingham). Universities more often thought of as campus universities may be more likely to be near a smaller town than a big city (for example, Lancaster and Warwick).

Other factors to consider

Attractiveness to employers

Few employers will openly admit to giving preference to graduates from particular universities. Most are looking for high-quality degrees as an indication of strong academic ability. But since students with higher A level grades have tended to go to the older and more prestigious univer- sities, it is unsurprising that a large proportion of successful lawyers come from these universities. Employers are often so swamped with applications that they use university background as an easy way to filter applicants, reckoning that the better universities will have picked the higher-calibre students and therefore have done part of their job for them. It therefore makes sense to be aware of the reputations of the different universities (which can often be gleaned from their position in the league tables) and factor this into your decision. You must obviously choose to go somewhere that you will enjoy, but since (at least part) of the object of the exercise is to find a good job at the end of your university studies, it is foolhardy to ignore how potential employers will view your degree.

Quality of teaching

This is difficult to establish without the benefit of an open day, and even then you will only have the opportunity to meet one or two of the teaching staff and speak to one or two students. However, league tables of universities for each subject are published by several organisations, such as the *Guardian*, the *Times and Sunday Times* and *The Complete University Guide*. The *Guardian University Guide 2018* for law is available online at www.theguardian.com/education/ng-interactive/2017/may/16/university-league-tables-2018 and the Complete University Guide 2017 Law league table is at www.thecompleteuniversityguide.co.uk/league-tables/rankings?s=Law. *The Times/Sunday Times Guide* is available in print format and is published annually.

The National Student Survey is conducted each year to get feedback from students who have studied at university, and is more focused on overall student satisfaction. Scores are given for many factors, including the quality of teaching and how good teachers are at providing feedback to students. The results of the survey are published online, including at www.hefce.ac.uk/lt/nss/results and on the website of Unistats: unistats.direct.gov.uk/find-out-more/about-the-data. Since the raising of tuition fees, students have become a lot more interested in issues such as teaching quality and 'contact time' – i.e. how much face-to-face teaching you will actually get, and it makes sense to investigate this as much as you can.

Teaching quality may suffer if seminar or tutorial groups are too large, so try to also compare group sizes for the same courses at different institutions.

Educational facilities

Most universities should have a well-stocked and up-to-date law library. They should also have good-quality IT resources and fast broadband internet connections. More vocational courses might also use mock courtrooms with video and audio equipment. The facilities available will depend on the budget of an institution, and obviously how they choose to spend it. You may want to look at the law department at the university. Is it in the new, shiny, state-of-the-art building or a dilapidated 1960s monstrosity hidden from view? At the end of the day, university is about more than just buildings – academically, the quality of teaching is more important and non-academic factors will also make a big difference to whether or not you enjoy your time there. However, if you are concerned about the environment in which you study, you should investigate the building housing the law department.

Non-academic considerations

- **Finances.** The cost of living differs substantially throughout the UK, so will you be able to reach deeper into your pockets for rent or other fundamentals and entertainment if you are living in a major city or in the south? If you are living in London, you will need particularly deep pockets.
- **Distance from home.** Do you want to get away from your family and friends or stay as close to them as possible? While there can be advantages, financially at least, to living at home if you go to your local university, you may prefer the challenge of looking after yourself and the opportunity to be completely independent. You should also think about whether you want to be able to go home at weekends without spending half a day (or more) on a train.
- **Accommodation.** What sort of accommodation is on offer? Do you want to live on campus or in halls of residence with other students, or in private housing that you may need to organise yourself that could be a considerable distance from college? Most universities provide accommodation for first year students at least, but how far this is from the teaching areas of the university will vary. You may simply be able to roll out of bed and totter next door for your 9am lectures, or you may be looking at a half-hour bus journey in rush hour. Some universities offer accommodation beyond the first year, which will save you having to live in private housing.
- **Catering.** Would you prefer to go somewhere where you can have your meals cooked for you, or are you keen to unleash your inner chef and cater for yourself?
- **Interests.** Will the university allow you to pursue your interests? Are you going to be spending much time in, for example, the sports centre, the theatre or student bars? How about university societies: is there one that allows you to indulge your existing hobbies or the ones you've always dreamt of trying? Most universities have a huge choice of extra-curricular activities and entertainments and very good facilities. However, you should think about exactly what is provided, the standard of participants and whether all abilities are catered for (are you a county squash player or simply keen to have a go?) and how far the facilities that you will want to use are from the accommodation or teaching areas. Some universities have particular reputations for particular extra-curricular activities – for example, Loughborough for sport.

Studying overseas and work placements

The opportunity to study overseas and/or complete a work placement could also be factors affecting your degree selection. Some universities will allow you to go to an overseas university with whom they have an arrangement for one year of your studies. Others will allow you to spend a year in the middle of your degree on a work placement. You do not need to be a linguist to study abroad, since you can study or work overseas in English in, for example, North America, the Netherlands or Malaysia.

The availability of student exchanges has increased through programmes such as Erasmus (an EU student exchange programme), which encourage universities to provide international opportunities where practicable. Despite the triggering of Article 50 and the initiation of the UK's exit from the European Union, the National Agency will continue to support the programme until at least 2020, covering the duration of the proposed Brexit implementation period.

If you are planning to study law at university, these opportunities may be more limited, as law is a very jurisdiction-specific subject.

Similarly, few law degree courses offer work placements during your degree. You will usually need to arrange this for during university holidays (see Chapter 5, page 74).

7 | The UCAS application and the LNAT

So you have chosen a few universities that you would like to apply to for a law degree; now what? This chapter will guide you through the UCAS application process for a law degree, and then give you some advice if you are applying to any universities that require the LNAT entrance exam.

Suggested application timescale

Lower Sixth

January onwards. Start doing some serious thinking and begin researching degree courses. Get ideas from friends, relatives, teachers, books, etc. Investigate (and book) one-day taster courses run by certain universities, such as those available with the University of London (see http://tasters.gradsintocareers.co.uk), and work experience for the summer holidays (see Chapter 5, page 74).

April. Find out when open days are being held (you may have to request universities you are interested in to notify you when bookings open). See www.opendays.com. Many are held in late June/July (after summer exams) and then again in September/October. It is helpful to do some in June/July if possible.

June/July. Attend open days. Look at university department websites, download prospectuses and department brochures.

July/August. Make a shortlist of your courses. Try to do as much research as possible over the summer holidays. This is particularly important for applicants to Oxford and Cambridge. Also, undertake work experience and wider reading (see suggestions in Chapter 12). Start writing your personal statement. Review your courses shortlist when you receive your summer exam results.

Upper Sixth

September onwards. Finalise your personal statement and UCAS form, then complete your application and send it off to UCAS. Register and book a place to sit the LNAT if you are applying to a university that uses it (see below).

15 October (6 p.m. UK time). Deadline for submitting your UCAS application if you are applying for places at Oxford or Cambridge.

20 October. Deadline for sitting the LNAT if you are applying to Oxford.

December. Interviews for Oxford and Cambridge are held.

15 January (6 p.m. UK time). Deadline for submitting your application to UCAS. They will consider late applications, but your chances are limited since some of the places will have gone already.

February – April. Interviews at non-Oxbridge universities may be held.

25 February – 4 July (6 p.m. UK time). If you have received decisions from all five of your choices, and were either rejected or have declined the offer you received from all of them, you can enter UCAS Extra, a scheme that allows you to apply to other universities, one at a time. See the UCAS website (www.ucas.com) for details.

November – March. Decisions (and hopefully, offers) arrive.

31 March. By this date, universities and colleges are encouraged to send UCAS their decisions on all applications received before 15 January.

2 May. If you have received all your university/college decisions by 31 March, assuming you've had some offers, you must tell UCAS which offer you have accepted firmly and which one is your insurance choice by this date.

June. Sit your exams.

August. (Third Thursday) Results day. If you got the grades, well done! UCAS will send you confirmation of your place. If you missed your grades, don't be too disappointed. Clearing starts straight away so don't waste any time – get hold of a list of unfilled places and contact the universities directly. You will be sent instructions on Clearing automatically. UCAS also runs a scheme called Adjustment which allows students who have performed significantly better than they had expected a short period of time to approach universities that require higher grades than the offer they were holding. See Chapter 10 for more information on your options on results day.

The UCAS form

The online UCAS form is accessed through the UCAS website (www.ucas.com). Most applicants register through their school or college, but it is possible to register independently. The UCAS form has six sections that you need to fill out.

1. Personal details: name, address, nationality, etc.
2. Choices: universities and courses you wish to apply for and your proposed year of entry.

3. Education: including exam results and exams to be taken.
4. Employment: including part-time work.
5. Personal statement: see below.
6. Reference: this is usually written by your school or college, but independent candidates can ask employers or other contacts to act as a referee.

General advice on filling in your UCAS application is given in another guide in this series, *How to Complete Your UCAS Application* (Trotman Education).

Your personal statement

The personal statement is the most important part of your UCAS application and is your opportunity to demonstrate that you are fully committed to studying law and have the right motivation and personal qualities to do so successfully. It is therefore vital that you think very carefully about how to complete it so that it shows you in the best possible light. You need to sell yourself to the law admissions tutors. It will take time and effort to get it right, so you must allow yourself plenty of time and not attempt to rush it. Expect to go through many drafts before you come up the final version that you are happy with.

There can often be over 20 applicants per place at some universities offering law degrees, so applying for a law degree is very competitive. A good personal statement can help you to stand out from the crowd and persuade an admissions tutor to give you an offer rather than one of the other equally well-qualified applicants.

Obviously, there are as many ways of writing a personal statement as there are candidates. There are no rules as such, but you should try and adhere to the following advice.

The personal statement should cover three key areas.

1. Why you want to study the course for which you are applying.
2. Why you would be good at the course and are well qualified to embark on it.
3. What other interests you have and (if possible) what transferable skills they give you which would be relevant for the course.

Section 3 should make up no more than 25% of the personal statement (or even less for the most academically competitive universities, such as Oxford, Cambridge and LSE). The focus should be on your academic interest in the courses applied for, and why you are a good candidate, and in most cases this should account for around 75% of the statement.

Some key points to remember.

● The personal statement must be no longer than 4,000 characters (including spaces). This is a strict limit, so you need to ensure that you do not exceed the character count.

● Write in your own words. The statement must be honest and personal and it must sound like you. After all, it is a *personal* statement, and admissions tutors will be using it to gain an insight into you as a potential student.

● Use evidence. Don't make broad-brush statements, but focus on what you have **actually done** and what you have learnt from it. Focus on how what you have done has helped you to decide a law degree is for you or to become a good candidate for a law degree.

● Check and re-check the statement for spelling, punctuation and grammar. Even better, ask a parent, teacher or family friend to do this for you.

● Do not over-use superlatives ('passion' etc.) although you should sound enthusiastic and committed.

Why you want to study law

The first part of the statement should show why you wish to study for a law degree. You can do this by providing answers to some of the following questions.

● Why do you wish to study law? Money, status or family traditions are not good reasons. Refer to evidence and the things that helped you reach your decision. For example: 'I am particularly interested in pursuing a career at the Bar. My enthusiasm was initially sparked by my active participation in the debating society at school, of which I am president. I found that I thoroughly enjoyed the challenge of putting across my point of view and trying to counteract the opposing argument.'

● What precisely is it about the law that interests you? Give details and examples, referring to recent cases and debates.

● Which particular area of law interests you most and, again, why?

● What related material have you recently read and why did you appreciate it? (See below for further guidance.)

● What legal cases have you followed and what recent judgements have you admired and why?

● What legal controversies have excited you? Are you up to date with current affairs and can you demonstrate your knowledge and understanding?

Well-chosen references to books you have read, including specific information you have gleaned from them, are very helpful. Some suggested reading for aspiring law students is contained in Chapter 12. Be careful not to just reel off a list of books – be specific about what interested you about them and what you learnt from them. You should also refer to any law taster courses you have attended but, again, don't just mention them – spell out what you gained from going to them and how they helped you decide that you would like to study law. You should also refer to any current legal issues appearing in the press and what you think of them or have learnt from them.

Work experience is very useful as it demonstrates a commitment to the subject outside the classroom, so mention any experience, paid or voluntary. Explain concisely what your job entailed and what you got out of the whole experience. Even if you haven't been able to get legal work experience, if you have spoken to anyone in the legal profession about their job, then it is worth mentioning as it all builds up a picture of someone who is keen and has done some research. Wanting to be like the characters in legal dramas on television is not enough, and neither is wanting to follow in a parent's footsteps!

Future plans, if any, should also be included on your form. Do not mention a desire to make a lot of money, since this is unlikely to impress admissions tutors who may well have shunned lucrative career opportunities in order to pursue an academic career.

Why you are a good candidate

You should also set out what makes you a good candidate for a law degree. If you have already explained why you wish to be a lawyer and how you made that decision, you will already have gone a long way towards demonstrating that you will be a committed student of the law. However, you should also briefly explain how your current school subjects (usually A levels) prepare you for studying a law degree. What skills have they allowed you to develop? If you have taken only maths and science A levels, you will need to describe how you are prepared for the more literary aspects of a law degree – i.e. reading and assimilating lots of information and preparing longer pieces of written work. You will also need to show that you can write an essay, so it would be a good idea to discuss any work you have carried out beyond your A levels, such as completion of the EPQ.

Extra-curricular activities and transferable skills

The last part of the statement should set out your extra-curricular activities, with a particular emphasis on what key transferable skills they have given you – for example, teamwork, self-motivation or leadership skills. If possible, you could try to link these in with the skills that will be necessary when studying for a law degree. If you are a school prefect, or team captain, then mention it here.

If you are planning to do so, state your reasons for applying for deferred entry and outline what you intend to do during your gap year. For example, you might be planning to find some relevant work experience in a firm of solicitors, and then spend some time overseas to brush up your language skills.

General advice

It is imperative that the focus of your personal statement is on the course of study that you wish to follow. Make sure that for each point you make, whether that be which A levels you are studying or the work experience that you have done, you are relating it back to the course.

Many universities now publish detailed advice about what they are looking for in a personal statement on their websites. You should carefully check the websites of all the universities you wish to apply to and make sure that you follow their advice. Most of it will simply be along the lines of the advice given above, but you should make sure you address any specific requirements or suggestions from the universities you are particularly interested in. You should also bear in mind the way that the universities describe the courses you are interested in on their websites. For example, if they emphasise the need for a practical approach, then it makes sense to highlight how you demonstrate an ability to be practical.

Finally, you should try to avoid some common pitfalls when writing your statement.

- Avoid cheesy clichés (e.g. 'for as long as I can remember') and over-use of quotations. One short quotation is acceptable if it is relevant and you comment on it.
- Do not include unsupported statements (e.g. 'I am hard-working'), which lack credibility. Instead, give evidence to support statements (e.g. things you have done which proved your capacity for hard work).
- Do not refer to specific courses as the same statement will go to all five of your university choices. You will not be able to write a convincing statement if you are applying to a variety of different courses (see below).
- Do not lie or exaggerate. You must be prepared to be asked on anything you mention in your statement if you are called for interview.
- Do not try to be funny. Humour is very personal and can easily be misinterpreted or backfire.
- Do not be tempted to get someone else (a friend, teacher, parent or one of the many internet sites that offer 'help') to write your personal statement. It has to sound like you, which is why it is called a personal statement.

> ## Caution!
>
> Never, ever, copy and paste any part of your statement from any other sources (whether from a friend or the examples in this book or somewhere online). UCAS runs all applications through anti-plagiarism software. If you do this, you will be caught out and your application will be void.

Make sure you print out a copy of your personal statement when you have finished it so that you can refer to it again and remind yourself of the points that you raised, should you be called for interview.

As emphasised in Chapter 1, it is not necessary to study law at university in order to become a lawyer (although it saves you a year of study). This chapter focuses on applying to university to study law, but if you are applying for a non-law degree, exactly the same issues arise. Your personal statement should focus on why you wish to study your particular subject at university and why you are a good candidate.

Warning: mixing courses and joint honours courses

You will write only one personal statement, which is read by admissions staff at the five courses for which you are applying, so you must make sure that it is suitable for all five courses. Each university sees only its name and course code on the form that UCAS sends to it: your other choices are not revealed. So, if you are applying to read psychology at one university (remember, you do not have to read law at university to become a lawyer), management at another, history at a third, and so on, then you cannot possibly write a personal statement that will satisfy the criteria for all of the courses. The psychology admissions tutor will wonder why you have written about history, and so on. The likelihood is that you will be rejected by all of your choices.

If you apply for a joint honours course such as law and French, your form will be seen by admissions tutors from both departments, each of whom will want to see that you are a serious candidate for his/her course. You must therefore cover both subjects in your statement.

Tips from admissions tutors

The following advice has all been given by law admissions tutors at leading university law schools over the last few years.

Admissions tutors want to see that you have a genuine reason for wanting to study law and have made your decision to apply for a law degree based on thorough research. You must show that you have thought carefully about why you want to study for a law degree and have properly researched the degree programmes you are applying for. Do not list your achievements without explaining their applicability to a law degree. You should also have an idea of the different areas of law you can work in, although it is perfectly acceptable not to have made up your mind yet about which area you would prefer.

You also need to show that you have a firm grasp of current affairs and regularly read a quality newspaper. An up-to-date understanding of the legal profession is also important. Some admissions tutors consider an awareness of current issues to be more important than reading law texts.

You should include any relevant work experience in your statement, although admissions tutors are very sensitive to the fact that not all students will have had the opportunity to get high-quality legal work experience. The general agenda to widen access to universities means that admissions tutors will make sure they avoid discriminating against applicants because of their background and the opportunities available to them. However, you still need to show what you have managed to do in the way of work experience and what you have learnt from it, even if it is not directly law related.

One important consideration for admissions tutors is the breadth of the application. In recent years, admissions tutors have commented on the fact that many applicants lack culture. While they may be committed to their studies or have undertaken a wealth of work experience, they don't often show their readiness to expand their knowledge, for example, by learning a new skill such as a language.

You should also:

- focus your personal statement on the course you are applying for
- make your personal statement sound like you
- apply early
- check carefully for spelling and grammatical errors.

Some sample personal statements for law degrees are shown below. Use these to get some ideas but **do not copy** any part of them into your own personal statement.

First sample personal statement *(3,892 characters)*

My interest in law began when I experienced the abuse of power by a law enforcement officer. Living in a country where corruption is rife, this was no surprise, but it made me question what would have happened without legal intervention. Following this, I sought experience at two prestigious Nigerian law firms with a track record for tackling social injustice. By undertaking internships at Banwo

---

and Ighodalo as well as Babalakin and Co., I became familiar with legal practice and furthered my knowledge of law in action by visiting both the Federal and Magistrate courts in Nigeria. Although many of the cases were based on relatively small financial matters, it demonstrated the importance of the judicial system in legitimising outcomes. I also explored financial matters during a taster course at SOAS University of London that concentrated on tort and contract law. This offered me greater insight into the legal system in the UK and furthered my desire to study law.

Studying essay-based subjects at A level, as well as an EPQ on the tenure of Goodluck Jonathan as President of Nigeria, I have developed the ability to make clear and unbiased judgements while considering multiple perspectives – skills intrinsic to the study of law. During my study of American history, civil rights in the United States and the existence of the Jim Crow laws stimulated my interest; I discovered the Plessy v. Ferguson case which introduced the 'separate but equal' doctrine legalising racial segregation. This remained in place until the ruling was overturned in 1954 in Brown v. Board of Education where the doctrine was deemed 'unconstitutional'. Irrespective of the fact that it did not immediately come into practice, this ruling was instrumental in securing the rights of African Americans, demonstrating to me the transformative powers of the law. I enjoyed scrutinising how, while the judiciary often work towards eradicating inequality, they can, on occasion, treat certain groups in an unfair manner. Helena Kennedy's Eve was Framed demonstrated to me how the legal system can perpetuate stereotypes. This notion that women often find the legal system difficult to navigate exemplified to me how I could utilise my law degree to help defend the human rights of those who have, historically, been treated in an unjust manner.

Studying biology has improved my analytical skills as I have been able to analyse evidence to determine its credibility and reliability. I have also explored a range of ethical issues, especially in the field of stem cell research. The questioning of morality was furthered through my reading of Hutchinson's Is Eating People Wrong?, which detailed the case of R v. Dudley and Stephens in which the defendants killed a cabin boy for food following a shipwreck; this set the precedent that necessity is not a defence to a murder case. My aptitude for evaluating quantitative aspects and my capacity to work logically are underpinned by my AS in maths.

Being events chair for the college debating team has heightened my organisational skills and enabled me to take part in a variety of debates, improving my ability to produce balanced and informed arguments. Recently, I debated the motion 'Brexit will have significant impact on international trade'. Using my background in economics, I analysed the EU laws and regulations and ultimately concluded that UK trade would diversify in terms of trading partners but would not necessarily be weakened.

I also took part in NCS: The Challenge whereby I managed several social action projects. I also play tennis at my local club, improving my ability to think well on my feet as it requires alertness and tactical thinking. As well as this, I recently commenced a language course in Mandarin. Through studying in the UK, I believe that my aspiration to become an international human rights lawyer will be one that I can achieve.

Second sample personal statement *(3,993 characters)*

Society is rife with inequities and it is the job of a lawyer to help eradicate them by protecting vulnerable members of our society. Being able to advocate for people who do not have access to justice is the main reason that I am interested in studying law. To expand my knowledge of the legal profession I have undertaken different work experience placements.

To understand the role of a barrister I have visited my local court. I was fascinated to observe how a barrister questioned the witnesses about minute details that would later impact the end result of the case. As this case was about police brutality it was also intriguing to learn how many other enquiries the case had undergone before being brought before the judge; it was later revealed that one of the reasons it had been brought to court was due to lobbying. This highlighted to me the importance of pressure groups in bringing forward cases that may have been overlooked by the judicial system. Work experience at Khan and Co., a high street law practice, has allowed me to see the inner workings of a smaller law firm; I sat in on a number of client meetings and watched the way in which the lawyers listened to their clients' legal issues, identified client needs and came up with solutions.

To gain insight into the corporate side of legal work I undertook work experience at Weightman's law firm; in the insurance department I helped to investigate a claim made by an employee against the company he was working for over a workplace injury. The difference between the two law firms was evident: Weightman's had access to many more resources than Khan and Co., and could use personnel from different departments within the firm.

Studying A level History has helped me to look at sources in an analytical way similar to that in which a lawyer would review evidence. An in-depth study of the magna carta has given me an appreciation of the basis of English common law and the long-lasting impact this historical document has had on our modern-day legal system. I have read *Letters to a Young Lawyer* by Alan Dershowitz, which highlights the issues of morality faced by lawyers throughout their careers. The book concludes that these challenges will be present throughout one's career but that every-one is entitled to justice and it is a lawyer's job to do their utmost to carry this out. Another text I found thought provoking was *Law and Religion in Multicultural Societies* by Mehdi et al. It outlines the changing views of religious and cultural practice within the law; through reading this book I appreciated the complexities involved in creating equal representation among all ethnic minorities as in many cases people view their own religious and cultural practices to be as binding as the law itself. These issues are ever more pres-ent as our culture becomes more diverse; a lawyer's ability to advocate for people of many different backgrounds is paramount to achieving fair and equal representation. In order to learn more about different cultures, I have taken part in Model United Nations, which has helped me to not only develop my debating skills but also to learn how to construct an argument, even when my own personal views do not match the views I am representing.

My voluntary work at a primary school and in organising sports training has taught me how to plan carefully, manage time, com-municate clearly and problem solve creatively. Volunteering at a nursing home for several months allowed me to observe at first hand the difficulties some people have in communicating their needs and, as an aspiring lawyer, I feel I have developed good social awareness through these experiences. I have cultivated important interpersonal skills by serving as vice captain on a netball team and being voted to participate in a sports committee. As a qualified lifeguard I have demonstrated that I can be trusted to undertake responsibility and undertake a leadership role.

Third sample personal statement *(3,987 characters)*

Harry Houdini once said that to study law is to perform tricks that even he can't figure out. As I have progressed through my A levels, I have found myself more drawn to the subject of law, especially as the cases are incredibly interesting. Studying law would allow me to pursue a career in a fast-paced and exciting field, while developing an incredibly diverse skill set. It also appeals to my hardworking and inquisitive nature. By talking to legal professionals, I have been able to acquire a strong understanding of what the route into law and the resulting career entails. Through these contacts, I have also been able to establish a range of work experience placements over the course of this academic year and during the summer in a wide range of legal environments. Now that my family are settled in the UK, I intend to pursue a career as a lawyer and work for a London firm, but hope that my studies will develop my understanding of the opportunities available in the UK and abroad.

I have held down numerous occupations over the last few years that have proven to be incredibly rewarding. While demonstrating my ability to manage my time carefully, it has also allowed me to develop effective skills in communication so that I can work with people from a diverse range of backgrounds. This was especially useful when I worked for the National Therapeutic Riding Association in Israel. Living in different places around the world has taught me the value of considering culture and has introduced me to the differences in the way that law is practised as a result. During my time in Israel, I attended a number of diplomatic events and this introduced me to a number of people in high-ranking positions, with whom I had to hold conversations about topics that were far beyond the expectations of someone my age. It gave me a real insight into many legal and political elements which led to my appreciation of the field. I have always focussed on the positives and learned whatever I can from my experiences of moving around.

My academic history was comprised predominantly of my time at Malvern College, a boarding school that I attended for 12 years. It was there that I was able to establish myself as a responsible leader by being given the prestigious titles of Head of Boarding and Head of Junior School. I was able to develop my communication skills through listening carefully to student concerns and presenting them to staff on behalf of my peers. I was successful in establishing numerous important changes as a result.

In my academic studies, I have always worked hard and strive for the best possible results. My A level studies lend themselves well to the subject of law. Naturally, studying law at A level has allowed me to grasp the basic understandings of the legal system and has given me a passion to learn more. Studying biology has allowed me to develop my approach to working with close attention to detail, as well as to analyse and evaluate sources of information presented in different ways. English literature has taught me the importance of context and how it affects how one may perceive a text, as well as allowing me to consider the suggestions of others and work critically.

I discovered how to work, listen, be happy and pick others up by participating in sports, and my most valuable lessons have been learnt by taking part in sporting teams. I was in Malvern College's 1st Netball Team from the age of 13, vice-captain at 16 and captain at 18, as well as being in the school's 1st Hockey team and the captain of Worcestershire County hockey team until I was selected to play for the Midlands regional team. Representing teams at such a high level has taught me the importance of working with integrity at all times and has allowed me to establish myself as a strong leader.

I look forward to pursuing a career in a field where I can support those who cannot defend themselves. As Charles Dickens stated, 'if there were no bad people, there would be no good lawyers'.

The LNAT

The LNAT is the National Admissions Test for Law. It is an externally set test which is used by a number of universities to help them select suitable candidates either for interview or for conditional offers. It does not test legal knowledge, but instead tests your aptitude for the skills required to study law, in particular:

- verbal reasoning
- ability to understand and interpret information
- ability to analyse information and draw conclusions
- deductive and inductive reasoning abilities.

The test lasts two-and-a-quarter hours and is in two sections – a multiple-choice section and an essay.

The multiple-choice section (95 minutes) is computer based and consists of 42 questions, based on passages of text setting out fictional scenarios. The score for this section is known as your LNAT score.

The essay section (40 minutes) tests your ability to construct logical, structured and clear arguments by writing one essay chosen from a list of essay questions. The essay is not actually marked by LNAT but is passed on to the participating universities with your LNAT score.

The best way to prepare yourself for the LNAT is to do several practice tests. The LNAT website (www.lnat.ac.uk) contains further details and also plenty of specimen questions and practice papers. There is also a practice test simulator that you can download. This is an on-screen simulation of the LNAT and includes a tutorial and two live practice tests. These will allow you to familiarise yourself with the format of the test and the skills it requires.

The multiple-choice section is based on fairly substantial passages of text, and examples of this section can be found on the LNAT website. However, below are some examples of the sort of essay questions you might be asked, with more examples available on the LNAT website.

1. In what circumstances should abortion be permitted and why?
2. Would you agree that travel and tourism exploit poorer nations and benefit only the richer ones?
3. Wearing a burkha in Western countries is just as offensive as wearing a bikini in Arab countries. Do you agree?

The LNAT is used by the following universities at the time of writing:

- Bristol
- Durham
- Glasgow
- King's College London
- Nottingham
- Oxford
- SOAS
- University College London.

(See below for details about the University of Cambridge.)

Registration for the LNAT opens on 1 August 2018, with testing beginning on 1 September 2018. The deadline for registering and booking the LNAT is 15 January 2019, and the test must be sat by 20 January 2019 (or 5 October and 20 October 2018 respectively for the University of Oxford). Further details can be found at www.lnat.ac.uk.

Other key points associated with the LNAT:

- The test is sat at an external test centre.
- The current cost of the test is £50 at UK and EU test centres, and £70 for other centres. The fee is payable online by credit or debit card at the time of booking.
- You can sit the test only once in any application cycle. If you sit it a second time, the later result will not count.
- If you reapply to universities that require the LNAT in subsequent years, you will have to sit the LNAT again.
- Candidates who may need extra time (for example, students with dyslexia) or need special arrangements (for example, students with sight or mobility problems) should register for the LNAT online, but should not book their test online. Documentary evidence must be supplied. Further information can be found on the LNAT website.

University of Cambridge

The University of Cambridge stopped using the LNAT test in 2010. It has replaced it with the Cambridge Law Test, which is used by nearly all Cambridge colleges. It consists of a one-hour paper that is normally sat when you attend for your interview. The questions do not require any prior knowledge of the law. The test is designed to ascertain a candidate's skills in comprehension and expression. Assessors will be looking to see how well the candidate engages with the question, the clarity of their written communication, logical presentation and a convincing argument. Details can be found on the University of Cambridge website (www.law.cam.ac.uk).

Case study

Ela secured excellent A level results, allowing her to take up her offer from LSE to study law. She is currently in her first year of the course.

'My first motivation to study law was my grandma. She is a practising lawyer and I was always interested in watching her work and learn about the cases she was involved in. This motivated me to apply for internships and I enjoyed them very much, so I decided that law was definitely the career I wanted to pursue.

'Having these experiences meant I was able to produce a strong personal statement, even though I didn't have any specific legal work experience. I tried to make it as concise as possible. My advice for the personal statement would be to get other people to read it, this would avoid you making avoidable mistakes and even simple grammatical errors that can be easy to miss when you've read your own work so many times! I also found it really helpful to read it aloud! It would be good to include any extra-curricular activities you have taken part in, but always remember to relate it to law and mention the transferable skills you have gained from them. Finally, don't expect the first draft to be perfect! It will take a few drafts to reach your ideal personal statement. I also carried out some wider research by reading introductory books and browsing university websites for recommended reading on areas that I found interesting.

'Preparing for the LNAT can be very time consuming, but the best thing to do is start preparing early. This will give you the chance to read any books that might be useful to develop your skills in critical thinking, as well as complete a lot of practice questions. If possible, try and get a teacher to mark them for you to give you an idea of how you are getting on.

'I am in the first term at LSE and have really enjoyed the study of criminal law, as the cases tend to be particularly interesting. The area that I have enjoyed the least at present is public law. Though I recognise it is really important, it is very theoretical and not very practical! There is a lot of work but this forces you to develop and utilise your time management skills so that you can stay on top of things. I have also joined a study group and this has made it much easier to stay on track with your reading!

'The lecturers have been really supportive at LSE and there are a lot of societies relating to law, which means that you meet a lot more people from the department. Some of them will have already been through the stage that you're currently at, so it is helpful to get their perspective on how to manage the workload and advice on reading material.

'Although I am only in my first year, I have identified some insight days and spring weeks at commercial law firms that I will attend. I am optimistic that these will allow me to secure a vacation scheme placement in my penultimate year. Eventually, I would like to gain a training contract at a City law firm, but I am enjoying the study of law so much that I would like to complete a master's degree in law first.'

8 | Succeeding at interview

Outside Oxford and Cambridge, formal interviews are rarely part of the admissions process for law degrees. Most universities, even those in the highly respected Russell Group of top universities, do not interview candidates for law degrees at all, other than those with unusual qualifications or mature students. In these cases, the universities interview because they need more information to help them make a decision. Interviews are expensive and time consuming for both the university and the applicants – as much of their programme delivery is based on problem-based learning, they use the interview as an opportunity to assess the relevant skills that cannot be demonstrated on the UCAS form. One notable exception at the time of writing is the University of York Law School, which does interview applicants – as much of their programme delivery is through problem-based learning, York uses the interview as an opportunity to assess the relevant skills that cannot be demonstrated on the UCAS form. Oxford and Cambridge also interview all applicants. If you are invited to attend an academic interview, this chapter contains some guidance on what to expect at the interview and how you might be able to prepare.

You may also be invited to an interview for work experience at a firm of solicitors or set of barristers' chambers. Much of the advice in this chapter is equally relevant to this situation and the same recommendations also apply. A few additional tips that apply particularly to interviews for work experience are given at the end of the chapter.

Oxbridge and York examples

Guides to interviews, including sample questions, and even video examples, are available on the websites of the universities of Oxford, Cambridge and York.

- www.ox.ac.uk/admissions/undergraduate/applying-to-oxford/interviews/interview-timetable?
- www.ox.ac.uk/admissions/undergraduate/applying-to-oxford/interviews/sample-interview-questions
- www.undergraduate.study.cam.ac.uk/applying/interviews
- www.york.ac.uk/law/undergraduate/interview

What to expect at the interview

The purpose of an interview is to test your:

- motivation to study law
- logical reasoning ability
- effective communication skills.

The university is not seeking to test your prior knowledge of the law.

You are likely to be asked questions on the following:

- why you wish to study law
- why you wish to go to that particular university
- your academic qualifications
- the personal statement in your UCAS form
- some questions on legal issues which are designed to assess your logical reasoning and communication skills.

You will also be asked whether there is anything you would like to ask your interviewer.

Interviews need not be daunting. They are designed to help those asking the questions to find out as much about you as they can. Interviewers are more interested in what you know than in what you do not.

The interview is a chance for you to demonstrate your knowledge of, commitment to and enthusiasm for the law. Interviewers clearly wish to know your reasons for wanting to study law and, possibly above all, they will be looking to see whether you have a mind capable of developing logical arguments and the ability to articulate such arguments powerfully and coherently. You should view an interview as a chance to put yourself across well rather than as an obstacle course designed to catch you out.

Preparation for a law interview

Once you have been asked to attend an interview, it is sensible to prepare thoroughly. You should take the time to think through your answers to some of the questions you are likely to be asked. You should also be very well informed about the course you are applying for and any current legal issues which you might be asked about. Try to arrange some mock interviews, carried out by a teacher at school, careers advisor, family friend, or anyone else you can persuade to help. These can be very useful. Reeling off pre-prepared answers to questions is obviously not going to impress an interviewer, but thinking in advance about what you are likely to be asked about can help you get your thoughts in order and sound confident and prepared at the interview.

Re-read your personal statement

You are very likely to be asked questions about your personal statement, so read it through well before the interview and make sure you can remember and speak coherently about any books you mentioned having read. If you have followed the advice contained in Chapter 7 of this book, you will not have included anything in your statement that you are not prepared to speak about at interview. Take a copy of the statement with you to the interview and read it through again shortly beforehand.

Why do you want to study law?

This is an obvious question and you should think about your reasons carefully before the interview. Reasons for wishing to study law vary. A passion for television courtroom drama series is not enough. You need to think about the everyday practice of the law in this country and it is very useful to spend time talking with lawyers of all kinds and learning what is involved. You may well be asked whether you have spoken to any lawyers about their work or visited any courts.

In terms of answering the question at interview, it is crucial that you convey a genuine interest in studying law. Often, your response will be in line with your personal statement. There are several possible aspects that you could cover when answering this question.

- An interest in law that has stemmed from a genuine interest in political affairs and the legal system. You might have followed some cases closely that you found particularly interesting, or read a book that piqued your interest. You need to be prepared to provide specifics here, and to answer questions on the things that you mention as evidence to support your answers.
- An event that occurred may have motivated you to pursue a degree or a career in law. This could be witnessing a lawyer represent someone you know, or perhaps even observing a perversion of the court of justice that you want to help overcome. It is important that these narratives are true, as you will need to be able to convey your resulting enthusiasm convincingly and be able to answer any related questions that an interviewer might have.
- It may have been a work experience placement or a conversation with a lawyer that stimulated your interest. You should consider exactly what it was that got your attention – a specific element of the work a lawyer was conducting that you found interesting, or a role that you were allowed to support with that you enjoyed. Lawyers can carry out a wide range of tasks, so reflect carefully on all elements of the job and the kind of environment in which they work.
- You may want to study law for the academic challenge that it represents as opposed to the career prospects. If this is the real

motivator, then you should consider the ways in which the course will stretch your capabilities and the skills that it will allow you to develop. Highlight any modules of particular interest, and explain why they interest you.

- The skills that you have may lend themselves well to the study of law, and reflecting on them at this point could strengthen your case. It is important to be modest, though – resist the urge to exaggerate!

It is important to be aware of the many types of law that lawyers practise – criminal, contract, family, taxation, etc. – and be clear about the differences between them. You may be asked what areas of law you are particularly interested in or whether you hope to become a barrister or solicitor (although you would not be expected to have come to any firm decisions at this stage). You should be clear in your mind about the difference between them.

Never talk about how much you expect to earn, or demonstrate any passivity about your decision to study law. Your parents making the suggestion for you to do so, following a family tradition or watching TV shows are unlikely to make a good case for obtaining an offer.

Many interviewers will also expect you to answer a question along the lines of 'Why should we offer you a place?' These questions often arise towards the end of an interview, and therefore provide a useful opportunity for you to summarise the key points that you have covered in your interview, highlighting the reasons why you want to study law, your skills, what you have to offer and reasons for choosing that particular university. It is also worth discussing how you might be able to contribute to other aspects of university life, including extra-curricular activities such as sports and music. It might also be useful to discuss any ways in which you have contributed to your school community, such as organising charity events or participating in clubs and societies.

Make sure you know all about the course and the university

Read through all the information on the university's website relevant to the course you have chosen and also read any brochures or other written information you may have been given at any open day you attended.

A common question early on in an interview is why you chose to apply for that particular university. It is important to look carefully at the information available on the course. If there is a particular element of the course that differs from others, reflect on it. For example, a university may have a very well established research department if you are interested in academia, while others may have a particular emphasis on work experience and provide good links to assist students in securing placements. Or there might be a specific module on offer, delivered by a specialist in the area, in which you have a particular interest.

The reputation of the department will typically be a determining factor in choosing a university, but it is also worth investigating the approach to teaching. Some of the more academic universities expect a greater degree of independent work, while others offer more support. Some universities deliver sessions using problem-based learning, which can be an excellent way of developing your skills, but it is not suitable for everyone.

Mentioning aspects such as the local excellent nightlife is not recommended, even if it did influence your decision initially! Law is an incredibly demanding course, and interviewers and admissions officers won't want to hear about potential distractions.

Practise getting the right body language

This is not as obvious as it seems, so a small amount of practice will make all the difference. Use mock interviews to give you some practice of walking into a room, looking your interviewer in the eyes, smiling, saying hello and shaking their hand. The handshake should be firm and confident – but without crushing their fingers. Sit down upright in your seat and do not slouch or lean back too far. You want to look interested and engaged and also relaxed, but not overly casual.

Be informed about current affairs

Reading a quality daily newspaper will keep you up to date with current legal issues and how they are reported in the media. Issues relating to politics, the police, sentencing and prison reform are possible interview topics.

Broadsheet newspapers, such as the *Independent, The Times* and the *Guardian* all report on current legal issues and give you insight into important legal cases. You could also read *The Law Society Gazette* or *The Lawyer*, which are published weekly in print format and are also available online. *The Law Society Gazette* contains reviews of current legal issues and matters affecting the legal profession. *The Lawyer* tends to focus more on news and comment about comings and goings in the legal profession (such as mergers between law firms).

Many current issues discussed on radio and television have legal implications. Watching or listening to *Question Time, Newsnight* and certain *Panorama*-style documentaries and Radio 4's *Today* programme, *The World This Weekend* and *Today in Parliament* will enable you to develop a thorough knowledge of current affairs. You could also visit the legal websites mentioned in the 'Further information' chapter at the end of the book.

In preparing for an interview, you should consider questions such as:

- what do you think should be happening in the prison system at the moment?
- what reforms would you like to see implemented in the running of the police force?

To be confident in presenting your opinions, it is helpful to discuss such issues with friends or family and then practise answering the questions at mock interviews.

In addition to discussing specific cases and legal reforms, it is highly likely that recent political events will form part of the interview. Politics can change rapidly – no one predicted a General Election in 2017, for example – so it is vital that you stay well informed.

Outlined below are themes prominent in the political and legal sphere at the time of writing. Remember, this is just a rough guide as opposed to an exhaustive list – it is up to you to stay abreast of current affairs.

Brexit

The negotiations of Brexit and the trajectory of the Great Repeal Bill should be closely followed by any prospective lawyer. You may be asked to discuss the impact of Brexit on parliamentary sovereignty and also on the UK's legal system. Aspects to consider include:

- the impact of the UK's decision to leave the EU on parliamentary sovereignty and the power of the judiciary
- the Miller case and its implications on parliamentary sovereignty and the legal landscape.

R (Miller) v. the Secretary of State for Exiting the European Union (2017) is a legal case where the UK Government was taken to court over its handling of Brexit. The premise of the case was that the Cabinet were neglecting the principle of parliamentary sovereignty as they made the decision to trigger Article 50 without a parliamentary vote. As a result of the court case, the UK's Supreme Court ruled there must be a vote within both chambers prior to triggering Article 50.

It is important to consider the implications of utilising legal frameworks to hold a government to account. You should consider the arguments for and against the decision of the plaintiff to launch the case.

It is also worth considering the media coverage for this particular case, with the tabloid Daily Mail dubbing the Supreme Court judges that came to the decision 'the enemies of the people', raising some interesting perceptions about the legal profession. Some might potentially view such judges as acting 'in ultra vires', or beyond one's power. You should consider whether unelected individuals should have the power to hold a government to account or not.

Environmentalism

With the Paris Accord (2014) established legal expectations regarding emissions reductions which all signatories must abide by. With the UK's fourth carbon budget fast approaching, environmentalism and the necessity of a low-carbon future are prominent themes at present. Concerns about the environment and air quality have intersected with the legal sphere, as seen by the multiple cases brought forward against the government by organisations such as ClientEarth. Some possible aspects to consider include the following.

- The culpability of governments with regards to air quality. You should consider whether or not you believe the government can be held liable.
- Issues associated with green crime and environmental laws and the challenges involved in deciding culpability and accountability.
- Whether the ClientEarth cases set a new legal precedent and what can be done in cases where there is no direct or clear victim.
- Cases brought against those who have protested using direct action, such as the Heathrow 13 or anti-fracking protestors.

The judicial branch in the USA

When appointed as 45th President of the United States, one of the first things that Donald Trump was able to do was appoint a member to the Supreme Court. This is a power that all US Presidents have held, yet their ability to use it depends entirely on a vacancy becoming available, either as a result of death, retirement or gross misconduct resulting in impeachment as Supreme Court justices are granted tenure for life. The life tenure raises concerns that the court could potentially serve as an echo chamber for presidential views, which could be indicative of the President having too much power.

Given that this differs significantly from the UK judicial system, it is certainly worth researching.

White-collar crime

Another area of interest is crime committed by the wealthy. These crimes are often corporate in nature and the term 'white-collar crime' can be applied.

As with green crimes, white-collar crimes are often difficult to prove as they tend to have no direct victim, and often there is very little delineation between legal and illegal behaviours. Take for instance the concepts of tax evasion and tax avoidance – one of them is completely legal, while the other is not.

There is a great degree of interest about how the wealthy and elite within society move their money, often as a means to avoid taxation. The widespread nature of such practices came to light in the Panama

Papers in 2015 and, more recently, in the Paradise Papers in 2017. It is well worth considering the legal implications of both these papers.

While exploring the low conviction rates for white-collar crime, it is worth considering the concerns that exist regarding the disproportionate number of working-class people within the prison population, and the ability of the upper classes to get away with criminal activity. Exploring this area could be augmented through researching the works of the theorists Snider and Chambliss.

Aspects to consider include:

● the administration of fair justice
● the issue of diversity in the legal preofession. Since law is the profession with the highest proportion of privately educated individuals, you could consider whether this may cause barriers to other individuals accessing the legal profession, as well a whether this lack of diversity has an impact on conviction rates.

Terrorism and anti-terror legislation

Concerns about the compatibility of the Human Rights Act with anti-terrorism legislation focus on how a major terrorist threat can be used to restrict people's civil rights and liberties. Consider whether you believe that human rights be suspended or limited in the face of a terrorist threat and how this interacts with the notion of judicial precedents. If contexts are constantly changing, is it better for the judiciary to consider things on a case-by-case basis?

Current affairs are constantly changing, which is why it is so important to stay up to date. Other aspects that are in the media at present include:

● cases pertaining to historic sex abuse
● prison riots and deaths in custody
● the effectiveness of different methids of administering justice: rehabilitative, retributive, punitive and restorative
● LGBT+ rights.

It is recommended that you add to this list as and when new topics present themselves in the news.

In addition to keeping a close eye on current affairs, compile a list of five to ten cases that you can discuss in both your personal statement and at interview. It would be a good idea to group these in themes. For example, the transformative power of the law regarding civil rights would be likely to include cases such as Brown v. Board of Education (1954); whereas cases regarding the rights of African Americans with Affirmative Action cases might include the recent case of Fisher v. University of Texas. Whichever cases you choose, ensure you know the facts and are able to express an informed opinion.

Joint degree subjects

If you have chosen a joint or combined honours course, then obviously you will have to prepare yourself for questions on the other subject you are hoping to study alongside law as well as questions on law.

Questions on legal issues

Knowledge of the structure of the legal and judicial systems is vital. Read Chapter 2 of this book to give you a basic understanding of the legal system. You should know who the Lord Chief Justice is, who the Director of Public Prosecutions is and what he or she does. You should be aware of recent controversial legal decisions, who took them and what their consequences are or could be. Who is the Home Secretary and why is he or she important?

Interviewers will ask questions with a view to being in a position to form an opinion about the quality of your thought and your ability to argue a particular case. You may be presented with a real or supposed set of circumstances and then be asked to comment on the legal implications of them. Is euthanasia wrong? What is the purpose of prison?

At the end of this chapter there are some sample questions, which show the type of legal questions you may be asked. Questions may be straightforward and specific, but can also involve more convoluted scenarios for you to think through. Remember that there are no right or wrong answers – you simply need to show that you can think through the issues in a logical and reasoned way and communicate your arguments and conclusions effectively.

On the day: practicalities and general advice

Arrive early

Make sure you know where you are going and leave plenty of time to get there. Allow for trains and buses to be delayed. Print off a map before you leave home and make sure you take the telephone number of the admissions office so that if, despite your best efforts, you are still late, you can phone and let them know. Remember to re-read your personal statement just before the interview.

Dress carefully

Dress comfortably, but show that you are taking the interview seriously: wear smart, clean clothes. Do not wear anything too revealing. You should also clean your shoes and make sure your hair is neat.

Be calm

Take a few deep breaths before the interview and, if you are nervous, try to calm and relax yourself. Listen to a favourite piece of music or something that you know will make you feel more relaxed. Remember you wouldn't have been invited for interview unless you were a serious candidate for a place, so be confident and let your talents shine through!

Demeanour during the interview

- Be yourself.
- Be enthusiastic and show a strong commitment to your subject.
- Maintain good eye contact with your interviewer(s) and confident body language.
- Listen carefully to the questions you are asked and make sure you understand what you are being asked before you answer. Don't be afraid to ask questions if you are unsure of what the interviewer wants.
- Be concise and logical – put forward your answer and use examples and factual knowledge to reinforce your points.
- If you are asked a question you don't know the answer to, say so. To waffle simply wastes time and lets you down. To lie, of course, is even worse – especially for aspiring lawyers!
- Be willing to consider new ideas, if your interview involves discussion of legal or other current issues. An ability to see the opposite point of view while maintaining your own will mark you out as strong law degree material.
- Show a willingness to learn and be prepared to admit defeat if you put forward an argument that is demolished by your interviewer. A touch of humility will not hurt.

An ability to think on your feet is vital – another prerequisite for a good lawyer. Although you will (hopefully) have thought through answers to some of the questions you are likely to be asked, you do not want to sound as though you are reeling off a pre-learned answer as this will sound false and will not impress anyone.

Much of the practice of law in this country rests on an adversarial system, so don't be surprised if you receive an adversarial interview.

Remember to keep calm and think clearly!

Think of some questions to ask your interviewer(s)

At the end of the interview, you will almost certainly be given the chance to ask if you have any questions. It is sensible to have one or two questions of a serious kind – to do with the course, the tuition and so on – up your sleeve. It is not wise, obviously, to ask them anything that you could and should have found out from the prospectus. If there is nothing, then say that your interview has covered all that you had thought of.

Above all, end on a positive note and remember to smile!

The interview for work experience

Most of the advice in this chapter will equally apply if you are going for an interview for work experience to a firm of solicitors or a set of chambers. However, in addition you should do the following.

- Research the firm/chambers thoroughly before interview. Look at their brochure and website.
- Plan in advance what you think your key selling points are to the employer and make sure you find an opportunity in the interview to get your points across.
- Prepare a few questions about the firm to ask your interviewer at the end. You can demonstrate your preparation here by asking them about something you have read about the firm/chambers recently, if appropriate.
- Dress smartly and appropriately. Lawyers tend to look quite formal, so a suit is probably appropriate in this situation.

Sample interview questions on legal issues

Here are a few sample legal questions which show the type of thing you may be asked.

1. Should cannabis/euthanasia be legalised?
2. What are the pros and cons of fusing the two branches of the legal profession?
3. Should the police in this country be armed?
4. If you were in a position of power, would you change the current civil legal aid situation?
5. Should the police spend their time enforcing the laws concerned with begging?
6. What do you think of recent law reforms?
7. What are your views on the right to silence?
8. How can you quantify compensation for victims of crime?
9. Should criminals be allowed to sell their stories as 'exclusives'?
10. Is it 'barbaric' to cane someone for vandalising cars?
11. How does the law affect your daily life?
12. What would happen if there were no law?
13. Is it necessary for the law to be entrenched in archaic tradition, ritual and jargon?

14. How are law and morality related?
15. Do you believe that all people have equal access to justice?
16. What is justice?
17. Why do we send criminals to prison? What are the alternatives?
18. Should the media be more careful with the way in which they report real crime?
19. Do you think the press should be allowed to report the names of celebrities when unproven allegations of sexual abuse have been made against them?
20. Is law the best way to handle situations such as domestic violence/child abuse/rape?
21. What causes crime rates to increase?
22. Is trial by jury a good idea? Should anyone be allowed to serve on a jury?
23. Do you think capital punishment should be reinstated?
24. Should the law permit suspected terrorists to be held indefinitely without trial?
25. If shop-lifting were punishable by death, and therefore nobody did it, would that be a just and effective law?
26. You are driving along a busy road with the window down when a swarm of bees flies into your car. You panic and lose control of the car, causing a huge pile-up. Are you legally responsible?
27. A blind person, travelling by train, gets out at his/her destination. Unfortunately the platform is shorter than the train, and the blind person falls to the ground, sustaining several injuries. Who, if anyone, should compensate him/her?
28. A cyclist rides the wrong way down a one-way street and a chimney falls on him. What legal proceedings should he take? What if he is riding down a private drive signed 'no trespassing'?

9 | Non-standard applications

Not everyone decides that they want to be a lawyer at an early age. Many successful lawyers are people who started out on a completely different career path. Equally, a number of successful lawyers in the UK come from overseas. Law firms and chambers welcome applicants from a wide range of backgrounds, and often have diversity initiatives in place. This chapter offers a brief overview of non-standard applications. For more information, please check with individual universities or the professional representative bodies for solicitors and barristers – i.e. the Law Societies of England and Wales, Scotland and Northern Ireland or, for aspiring barristers, the Bar Council of England and Wales, the Faculty of Advocates in Scotland or the Bar of Northern Ireland. Website addresses for all these institutions are given in Chapter 12.

Graduates with degrees other than law

Many lawyers, particularly in England and Wales, have obtained a degree in a subject other than law. As is explained more fully in the relevant sections of Chapter 4, this simply necessitates taking a further post-graduate qualification in law in order to cover the material that would usually be studied during a law degree. This qualification is the GDL in England and Wales, a two-year accelerated law degree in Scotland and a Masters in Law in Northern Ireland. The additional qualification is taken before moving on to the vocational stage of training. Please see the relevant sections of Chapter 4 for more information. Many employers positively welcome applications from non-law graduates, with the different range of skills that they bring. There are, however, financial implications as an extra year (two in Scotland) of study will need to be funded.

Mature students

Many law firms and sets of chambers positively welcome new recruits who are embarking on law as a second career. Experience or knowledge of particular business or industry sectors which form a law firm's client base can be especially welcomed. For example, former medical practitioners have the knowledge and experience to become excellent medical negligence lawyers. Many lawyers have not gone straight from school and university to the legal profession.

The possible routes for mature students to enter the legal professions depends on their level of academic qualifications.

Mature students who have a degree in a subject other than law are in the same position as other non-law graduates (discussed above) and are eligible to apply for the GDL or its equivalent outside England and Wales.

Mature students who do not have a degree can, if they can satisfy the entry requirements (i.e. they have A level or equivalent qualifications), simply apply to university as a mature student to obtain the necessary degree. If you are in this situation, it would make sense to make sure that your chosen degree is a QLD (see Chapter 4, page 46 for more details) to ensure that it will satisfy the academic stage of legal training and allow you to move straight on to the vocational stage of training (which is also summarised in Chapter 4).

Mature students without A levels (or equivalent qualifications) would need to take an Access to Higher Education course at a local further education college before applying to university. Each year around 20,000 Access to HE students apply for a degree course at a UK university to study subjects including law. These courses are outlined on page 45 in the section in Chapter 4 relating to England and Wales. In Scotland, a different system, called the Scottish Wider Access Programme, operates and Northern Irish universities have their own arrangements for access courses. More details are available at www. accesstohe.ac.uk.

Some universities offer QLDs with a Foundation year. These courses are designed to allow prospective lawyers without formal qualifications to gain access onto the course. The requirements for entry vary between universities, but applications tend to be considered from those who have completed the Access to Higher Education course, mature learners with no formal qualifications and young learners who have not undertaken post-16 qualifications. A list of providers and their entry requirements can be found on the UCAS website.

Alternatively, there are non-graduate routes to becoming a lawyer and these are also outlined in the relevant sections of Chapter 4. For example, the solicitors' profession in England and Wales offers a number of non-graduate entry routes, which are summarised in Figure 1 on page 44 and then explained more fully on page 49. Non-graduate routes to qualifying are also available in Scotland (see page 58) and Northern Ireland (see page 61).

Overseas students

Overseas students who already have a degree in their own country may apply to either the Solicitors Regulation Authority (for aspiring solicitors) or the Bar Standards Board (for barristers) for a certificate of academic standing, which will then allow them to take the GDL in England and Wales, in the same way as non-law graduates (see above).

Alternatively, overseas students might wish to start their training to become a UK lawyer by applying to study for their degree at a UK university. If you are in this situation, then the advice and guidance contained in Chapters 6 and 7 applies equally to you. However, the statistics show that overseas students are a lot less successful than UK students in gaining places at UK universities to read law, as the Law Society's figures for 2014 entry show:

Applicants' nationality	Number of applicants	Places	% Success
UK	25,155	17,855	71%
Overseas	9,120	4,910	54%

Table 5: Nationality and success rate for university law degree courses

This section therefore includes particular advice for overseas applicants on applying to a UK university to read law.

The process of applying as an international student is similar to that used by UK students: you use the same online UCAS form, provide the same information, and have the same deadlines. The differences are likely to be these:

- the examinations you have taken and/or will be taking may not appear in the drop-down menus on the UCAS form
- the fee codes and support arrangements will be different
- your school may not have registered with UCAS and so you may have to apply as a private individual rather than through an institution.

Detailed advice about how to fill in the UCAS form, and to deal with these issues, can be found in the 'Apply' section of the UCAS website (www.ucas.com). This section of the UCAS website contains special advice for international students for each section of the UCAS form. There is also a summary of tips for international students (www.ucas.com/ucas/undergraduate/getting-started/international-and-eu-students/tips-international-applications).

However, many well-qualified, serious and motivated international students are unsuccessful in their applications because they or their referees (or both) are unfamiliar with what the university selectors are looking for in two particular sections of the application form:

1. the personal statement
2. the reference.

The personal statement

Students who have applied for universities outside of the UK may be familiar with the idea of writing a statement about themselves to support their applications. These can often take the form of a 'hard sell', in which the student extols his or her personal qualities, achievements, hopes and dreams. This format is not suitable for a UCAS personal statement, which needs to focus on the course itself, and what the student has done to investigate it. The advice given in Chapter 7 is equally applicable to international students, and you should read it carefully. The UCAS website also recommends that you should specifically mention in your personal statement why you want to study in the UK, your English language skills (and any tests or courses you have taken) and why you do not want to study in your own country.

The reference

Often, a promising application is rejected because the person providing the reference is unfamiliar with what is required, and the selectors have no choice other than to reject because they are not given enough information. UCAS references need to focus on the following:

- the student's suitability for the course and level of study
- an assessment of the student's academic performance to date (including the student's level of English if this is not his or her first language)
- how the student will adapt to studying in the UK
- the student's personal qualities.

If you are unsure as to whether the person who will write your reference fully understands what is required, show them the section on the UCAS website called 'How to write UCAS undergraduate references': www.ucas.com/advisers/references/how-write-ucas-undergraduate-references.

LNAT

Some universities require candidates to sit the Law National Admissions Test (LNAT) in addition to gaining academic qualifications. This online test can be sat outside of the UK. See Chapter 7, pages 106–107 for more details.

Academic qualifications

The UCAS website (www.ucas.com) gives details of the acceptable non-UK qualifications. The international sections on individual university websites will provide further details. International students whose local qualifications are not acceptable to UK universities will need to study A levels or the equivalent either at an international school in their own country or at a school or college in the UK, or possibly follow a one-year university Foundation course. Details of providers of UK qualifications can be found on the British Council website (www.educationuk.org/global/articles/further-education-institutions).

Case study

Cameron grew up and studied in Perth, Western Australia. He is currently studying for his QLTS in order to transfer his qualifications and be admitted as a solicitor in England and Wales.

'Out of high school, I wasn't clear on the career I wanted to pursue, and was drawn to the various legal and non-legal options that a law degree can offer. I was also drawn to learning about writing and drafting, government and politics and how businesses operate generally.

'Out of university, I was interested more in the commercial side of things, and worked in logistics and procurement. It took some time before I decided to pursue a career in law, and to complete practical legal studies in order to be admitted as a solicitor in Western Australia. A few years ago, I moved from Australia to the UK, and have been working as an in-house legal advisor since arriving. I am now studying for the QLTS in order to transfer my qualifications and be admitted as a solicitor in England and Wales.

'My current role involves working closely with business stakeholders to negotiate client and supplier contracts, as well as reviewing and implementing internal policies and procedures to ensure regulatory and procedural compliance. In addition, my role also involves protecting the business from risk.

'To be successful in law, it is really important to identify the areas that you find most interesting. Getting involved is the best way of moving forward in that field as gaining hands-on experience will allow you to develop your knowledge of the area and to gain practical skills at the same time.'

10 | Results day

A level results day is arguably one of the most important days of your life, but don't panic: this chapter will provide you with some calm and practical advice on what to do on the day, whatever your results are.

The A level results will arrive at your school on the third Thursday in August. The universities will have received them a few days earlier. It is much better for you to go into school in person on the day the results are published, so do not arrange to be away on holiday then. Do not wait for the results slip to be posted to you. Try to get hold of your results as soon as possible on the day – if you need to act to secure your place or go through Clearing, then time is of the essence as you will be competing with other students in the same situation.

If you live overseas and are unable to go into school, make sure that you get hold of your results in some other way as soon as possible on results day.

Hopefully, you will need to do nothing other than celebrate! If you have a conditional offer and your grades equal or exceed that offer, then you can relax and wait for your chosen university to send you joining instructions. To check that all is in order, you can log on to the 'Track' facility on the UCAS website to make sure that your place has been confirmed.

> **Caution!**
>
> You cannot assume that equivalent grades such as A*AB will satisfy an AAA offer. Always check with your chosen university.

If your results are not as good as you had expected, or better than you expected, or you did not receive an offer from any of your chosen universities, then there are a number of options.

What to do if your grades are significantly better than anticipated

You may have significantly beaten the terms of your firm offer and now think that you might like to go somewhere 'better'. UCAS now uses a scheme called Adjustment, which is aimed at applicants who achieved better grades than predicted. It is primarily designed for students who might have been predicted low grades and therefore applied to universities that would accept them rather than those where they would really like to study. The Adjustment system allows you to put your existing firm offer on hold for a short period of time (five days) while contacting other universities where the standard offers are higher to see whether they will offer you a place with your higher grades. If you do not secure a new offer within this time period, or if you do not like what else is available, your original firm offer still stands and can still be accepted. Full details can be found on the UCAS website.

Alternatively, you may choose to withdraw from UCAS and reapply the following year with your higher grades.

What to do if you hold an offer but miss the grades

If you have only narrowly missed the required grades (either for your 'firm' or 'insurance' choice), it is important that you and your referee contact the university as soon as possible on results day, because you may be able to persuade the university to consider you.

If you miss the grades for your firm choice, but meet the grades for your insurance choice, you will automatically be accepted onto the insurance place. You can still contact your first choice institution to see whether or not it will accept you.

If you do not achieve the grades required for either your firm or insurance choice, and you are unable to persuade either university still to accept you, then you are eligible to enter Clearing. This is a list of places that are still available on various courses at all of the universities. The list is published in national newspapers and on the UCAS website. Places on law degrees available through Clearing will be few and far between, but if there is a place available at a university you would be interested in going to, then you must contact the university by telephone as quickly as possible on results day, because you will be competing with other students in the same position. Clearing is a stressful system and you must make your decisions carefully and in a measured way despite the time pressure. There is no point in accepting a place at a university where you do not realistically want to study.

In reality, due to the popularity of law as a degree, you should not pin your hopes on obtaining an offer of a place through Clearing. You may find that despite your best efforts, there simply are not any places available on law courses at universities where you would want to study. If you are unable to obtain a suitable place through Clearing, your best option would be to withdraw from UCAS altogether and then wait and reapply in the next academic year to courses for which you meet the entry requirements, with the benefit of your A level results to support your application. Given what has been said about the importance of choosing your university law course in Chapter 6, you do not want to settle for any university just because it has a place available, but hold out for a place at a university you are actually really enthusiastic about attending. In the meantime, you can use the time constructively by getting some work experience to build up your CV. You may also want to consider retaking some or all of your A levels in order to improve your chances of getting into a university you are really interested in going to.

What to do if you have no offer

If you did not receive any offers, you may have managed to find an offer through UCAS Extra. This scheme allows you to apply to other universities, either for law or for other courses. You will automatically be sent details by UCAS. UCAS Extra starts in February. If UCAS Extra does not provide you with an offer, you can enter Clearing in August once you have your results – see the details on Clearing above.

However, if you did not receive any offers when you applied, perhaps because your predicted results were not particularly strong, but you have ended up with better A level results than expected, then you need to make universities aware of this. Try to get in touch with them as early as possible on results day to see if they will reconsider their decision in the light of your results. The best way to do this is by telephone and email, and your UCAS referee may be able to help you in this respect. Try to persuade your referee to ring the admissions officers on your behalf – they will find it easier to get through than you will – or to email a note in support of your application.

Retaking your A levels

This may be a sensible option for students who know they are capable of achieving better grades than they did first time round. However, you should be aware that the grade requirements for retake candidates are often higher than for first-timers. You should investigate the particular universities you are interested in to find out what they require from retake students.

Independent sixth-form colleges provide specialist advice and teaching for students considering A level retakes. Interviews to discuss this are free and carry no obligation to enrol on a course, so it is worth taking the time to talk to their staff before you make any final decisions. Many will be able to give advice on results day if necessary.

Extenuating circumstances

If your grades were below those that were predicted or expected because of extenuating circumstances such as illness or family problems during exam time, make sure that you have written confirmation of this (such as a letter from a doctor, solicitor or someone at your school or college) and send this to the admissions department for your chosen course. The extenuating circumstances should be serious enough to merit special consideration and not just minor irritations.

Ideally, if something does go wrong at the time you are sitting your exams, you or your school/college should inform the universities immediately, warning them that you might not achieve the grades. It is more likely that they can make concessions then rather than when they have already made decisions about who to accept when the results are issued. For extenuating circumstances to be considered, universities often expect evidence to have been submitted to the relevant exam board for the affected exam.

Case study

Having missed his grades first time around, Peter showed true determination by repeating some of his A levels to ensure he reached his academic potential, allowing him to secure a place to study law at the University of Birmingham.

'It was my combined interest in business and the legal sector that encouraged me to pursue a career in law. I wanted to work in a corporate environment but obtain a degree that would provide me with many skills and a specific career route, so law seemed like the perfect option.

'During the course of my degree, I attended some open days at commercial law firms where I could talk to lawyers, form new contacts and ask questions to get a real insight into what the role would entail. This gave me all of the information I needed to establish that this was the area I wanted to pursue.

'The advice I received was to gain hands-on experience, so I undertook a vacation scheme. This proved to be invaluable as I really got a feel for the day-to-day demands and the type of work that I would be doing. It also gave me a lot to talk about when applying for training contracts and attending interviews. While the firms looked at many areas, including academic success, there is no doubt that the vacation scheme gave me the knowledge and the confidence to talk and reflect in depth. I also worked part-time

---

throughout my degree – it was raised in my interview and was crucial in my success, as the interviewers were keen to see how well I worked with other people, how I managed difficult situations and how I balanced my time.

'I am now working for Berwin Leighton Paisner, an international commercial law firm in London.'

Students with disabilities and special educational needs

For the most part, universities are able to accommodate students with a wide range of disabilities and special educational needs. As such, they are encouraged to apply to study law. On the UCAS form, there is a section that allows students to disclose such information, and it is recommended that a full description of the disabilities or special educational needs are provided, as well as the support required. All institutions are committed to supporting students with such considerations, but it is always worth contacting each institution and, where possible, the specific department, to determine how much support they will be able to offer. Most institutions well have a dedicated team of equality and diversity advisors employed solely to provide guidance and support.

When you receive an offer from a university, they should follow up with you directly regarding the disabilities outlined on your UCAS form. It is vital that you ensure there is complete transparency at this stage, as a lack of coherency or failure to reveal a full picture may result in complications in securing appropriate accommodation and could even result in withdrawal from the course.

It is also worth considering how accessible a career in law is for someone with a disability. The Equality Act (2010) has ensured that workplaces put the appropriate measures in place, as much as possible, to allow disabled people to thrive in the workplace. In theory, there is no barrier to working as a lawyer with a physical disability, though it is evident that not all workplaces will be suitable. Large solicitors' firms, for example, are likely to comprise appropriate disability measures such as lifts and adapted entrances and exits, whereas smaller firms may not have the means to adjust.

Students with special educational needs who require support in the form of additional time in exams, for example, will need to provide the appropriate supporting documentation. As long as this can be provided, there should be no issues in securing these access arrangements.

11 | Fees and funding

Seeking to qualify as a lawyer is expensive: first (usually) you have to fund a university degree and then you need to fund the vocational stage of training (possibly preceded by a postgraduate qualification in law, such as the GDL in England and Wales, if your degree was not in law). This chapter looks at the fees for the university degree stage of qualification and how those fees are funded. The fees and funding arrangements for postgraduate studies in law and the vocational stage of training depend on whether you wish to qualify as a solicitor or barrister, the qualification route you choose, and the jurisdiction within which you live. The fees and funding arrangements for these courses are therefore discussed in Chapter 4 under the relevant headings for the different qualifications. This chapter briefly outlines the current fee structure for UK universities and the way in which the governments of the constituent countries of the UK help students fund their university studies. More information can be found at www.gov.uk/student-finance.

UK students

Universities in the UK can charge students up to £9,250 a year in tuition fees, and most of the higher-ranked universities in England charge the maximum amount. Private colleges and universities are not subject to the £9,250 maximum, so can charge more. In most cases, these fees are not actually charged directly to students as the vast majority of students take out a student loan, which is repayable only after graduation and only once certain salary thresholds are reached (see below). There are different fee structures and different types and levels of financial assistance available, depending on which part of the UK you are from and where you choose to study. These are briefly summarised below, but you should check the websites of individual universities for specific fees and visit the recommended government websites below for more information about student finance.

English residents

English students will pay tuition fees of up to £9,250 wherever they study in the UK for the 2017/2018 academic year, and this is likely to increase with inflation for the 2018/2019 cycle. A tuition fee loan is available to cover these fees in their entirety. If you are applying to study at a private university, a loan of £6,165 is available to support with paying the tuition fees.

Also available are maintenance loans to cover your living expenses while you are at university. The amount of maintenance loan is income-assessed. The guaranteed portion of the loan (which is less than half) is available to all students, but those from lower-income households are able to borrow higher amounts on a sliding scale up to the maximum loan available (which is £7,097 for students living at home, £8,430 for those studying outside London and £11,002 for those studying in London for 2017/2018).

The tuition fee loan and the maintenance loan are repayable via the income tax system only after you have graduated and only if and when you are earning more than £21,000. Once your income exceeds this value, you will pay 9% of anything that you earn above £21,000. The repayments are a fixed part of your income and therefore depend on your future earnings and not on the size of your loan. All remaining debt is wiped after 30 years if it has not been fully repaid by then.

Student loan applications are made through the Government's Student Finance website: www.gov.uk/apply-online-for-student-finance. You apply for student finance for the 2018/2019 academic year in 2018. The deadline for applying is nine months after the start of the academic year.

Welsh residents

Welsh students will also be charged up to £9,250 wherever they study in the UK. However, regardless of where in the UK they study, they are entitled to a fee grant from the Welsh Government of up to £4,954 a year (for 2017 starters) towards their tuition fees. The remainder of their tuition fees will be funded by a tuition fee loan and the grant will then cover the difference between the loan and the amount charged by the student's university. The rules for living expenses and maintenance loans also differ from those in England. For more information on fees and student finance available in Wales visit www.studentfinancewales.co.uk.

Northern Ireland residents

Northern Irish students will pay up to £9,250 per year tuition fees if they study in England, Wales or Scotland, but will pay a reduced fee (£4,030 for 2017 starters) if they study in Northern Ireland. For more information on fees and student finance available in Northern Ireland visit www.studentfinanceni.co.uk.

Scottish residents

Scottish students will not pay any tuition fees if they go to a Scottish university, but they will pay up to £9,250 if they study anywhere else in the UK. The rules for help with funding living expenses differ from those in England and there are some living-costs grants available for students from lower-income households. For more information on fees and student finance available in Scotland visit the website of the Student Awards Agency Scotland: www.saas.gov.uk.

EU students

Students from other EU countries will be charged up to £9,250 if they study in England, Wales or Northern Ireland, but will not pay fees if they study in Scotland. The relevant funding bodies have all confirmed that EU funding will remain in place for the 2018/2019 admissions cycle, though owing to the impending exit of the UK from the EU, the funding status from this point onwards is currently unconfirmed. For more information about tuition fees and student finance available for EU students visit the relevant government websites (listed above) as well as the finance pages on individual university websites.

Non-EU international students

The fees for non-EU students do not have an upper limit and will depend on the course and the university. International students should contact individual universities for information on the fees they will be charging non-EU students. For more information visit the website of the UK Council for International Student Affairs, which also has advice on student visa applications: www.ukcisa.org.uk.

Bursaries and scholarships

UK universities now offer a wide range of bursaries and scholarships to support some of their students. In order to charge the maximum permitted tuition fees of £9,250, universities must prove that they are awarding bursaries to poorer students. These are contributions towards the cost of going to university that do not have to be repaid. The terms of these will vary between the universities and you should check the universities' websites carefully to see whether you may be able to apply for any financial help. Usually, bursaries are completely dependent on your household income, whereas scholarships are at least partly dependent on academic or extra-curricular (e.g. sporting) ability.

Funding the GDL, LPC and BPTC

GDL

The GDL is an expensive but unavoidable way of qualifying as a lawyer for graduates without QLDs. Unfortunately, postgraduate funding is not an option for covering GDL fees, but there are a number of ways of providing financial support. Often, GDL students will need to combine a number of sources of funding to pay the fees and support themselves for the duration. Some providers recognise the cost implications and now offer part-time courses and instalment payment plans, so research the stance of the provider on this when applying.

Perhaps the most obvious way to secure funding is to determine whether the GDL provider offers any scholarships or bursaries. You need to be on the ball with these, as they tend to be competitive with early deadlines. Many law firms will offer to cover the fees of the GDL if a training contract is secured early, with some even providing a maintenance grant to support with living costs. Some will even pay retrospectively if a training contract is secured mid-GDL, but the stance of law firms doing so is highly variable, so research carefully and check with them directly. The Law Society also offers a bursary scheme and these are awarded on the applicant's merit.

Graduate loans are also available up to the value of £15,000 through high street banks. These are not always ideal as repayments often start immediately, so be sure to exhaust all other options first.

LPC

As with the GDL, the LPC is a costly but crucial element of qualifying as a solicitor. Many of the funding options are the same as with the GDL, with the option of part-time study being popular as it allows students to work part-time, too. Scholarships and bursaries will be available from course providers and the Law Society, including the DAS scheme (as outlined in Chapter 4), and law firms will often fund your training once you have secured a training contract. In addition, studying the LPC qualifies for a Professional Career and Development Loan of up to £10,000, with repayments beginning one month after completion.

Though Student Finance Postgraduate Loans do not cover a standard LPC, the University of Law has now started offering master's degrees in law with integrated LPCs, thereby qualifying the training for this source of funding. This will mean that your fees are covered, and you will complete both the LPC and a master's degree simultaneously, so it is certainly worth consideration!

BPTC

Scholarships for the BPTC can be accessed through the Inns of Court, and these are the most significant sources of funding for this particular stage of training. Some chambers offer pupillage awards if a pupillage is secured prior to the commencement of the BPTC, but this is quite rare. The BPTC can also be funded using a Professional Career and Development Loan, though it is recommended that all scholarship options are researched first.

12| Further information

Useful websites

Legal professions

Solicitors

The Law Society (of England and Wales): www.lawsociety.org.uk
Statistics:
www.lawsociety.org.uk/policy-campaigns/research-trends/annual-statistical-reports

Solicitors Regulation Authority: www.sra.org.uk

The Law Society of Scotland: www.lawscot.org.uk

The Law Society of Northern Ireland: www.lawsoc-ni.org

Barristers

The Bar Council of England and Wales: www.barcouncil.org.uk

The Bar Standards Board: www.barstandardsboard.org.uk
Statistics:
www.barstandardsboard.org.uk/media-centre/research-and-statistics
www.barstandardsboard.org.uk/media/1599997/bsb_barometer_report_112pp_june_13.pdf

Gray's Inn: www.graysinn.org.uk

The Inner Temple: www.innertemple.org.uk

Lincoln's Inn: www.lincolnsinn.org.uk

The Middle Temple: www.middletemple.org.uk

The Faculty of Advocates in Scotland: www.advocates.org.uk

Northern Ireland Bar: www.barofni.com

Other legal professions

Legal executives: www.cilex.org.uk

Paralegals: www.theiop.org

Licensed conveyancers: www.clc-uk.org

Notaries: www.thenotariessociety.org.uk

Law costs draftsmen: www.associationofcostslawyers.co.uk

Trademark agents: www.citma.org.uk/home

Patent agents: www.cipa.org.uk

Legal secretaries: www.institutelegalsecretaries.com

Legal profession: directories

Chambers UK and Chambers UK Bar Guide: www.chambersand
partners.com
(Chambers publishes comprehensive online directories, containing
ranking tables and commentary, of firms of solicitors and barristers'
chambers. They are also published annually in print format.)

Legal 500: www.legal500.com
(An in-depth survey of the UK legal profession, also published annually
in print format.)

TARGETjobs: https://targetjobs.co.uk/careers-products
(TARGETjobs publishes online graduate careers guides and directories
for various professions including law:
    TARGETjobs: Law
    TARGETjobs: Law vacation schemes & Mini pupillages
    TARGETjobs: Law Pupillages Handbook.)

Law firms gossip: www.rollonfriday.com

Legal systems

Ministry of Justice: www.justice.gov.uk

Wales: www.assemblywales.org

Scotland: www.scotcourts.gov.uk/about-the-scottish-court-service

Northern Ireland:
www.niassembly.gov.uk
www.gov.uk/guidance/devolution-settlement-northern-ireland
www.nidirect.gov.uk/information-and-services/crime-justice-and-law

Other legal organisations

Crown Prosecution Service: www.cps.gov.uk

Legal Action Group: www.lag.org.uk

Education and training

A levels

Russell Group: www.russellgroup.ac.uk/informed-choices.aspx

UK qualification providers overseas: https://study-uk.britishcouncil.org

Access to Higher Education courses: www.accesstohe.ac.uk

University applications

UCAS: www.ucas.com
>UCAS Parent Guide (information about the UCAS undergraduate application process): www.ucas.com/ucas/undergraduate/getting-started/ucas-undergraduate-parents-and-guardians
>UCAS reference: www.ucas.com/advisers/references/how-write-ucas-undergraduate-references

University guides:
www.thecompleteuniversityguide.co.uk
www.theguardian.com/education/ng-interactive/2017/may/16/university-league-tables-2018

LNAT: www.lnat.ac.uk

University of Cambridge law: www.law.cam.ac.uk

University open days:www.opendays.com

Law interviews

Oxford:
www.ox.ac.uk/admissions/undergraduate/applying-to-oxford/interviews/interview-timetable
www.ox.ac.uk/admissions/undergraduate/applying-to-oxford/interviews/sample-interview-questions

Cambridge: www.undergraduate.study.cam.ac.uk/applying/interviews

York: www.york.ac.uk/law/undergraduate/interview

Fees and funding

UK: www.gov.uk/student-finance

Wales: www.studentfinancewales.co.uk

Scotland: www.saas.gov.uk

Northern Ireland: www.studentfinanceni.co.uk

Overseas students: www.ukcisa.org.uk

Vocational training

GDL course providers: www.sra.org.uk/students/courses/cpe-gdl-course-providers.page

Central Applications Board (for GDL and LPC): www.lawcabs.ac.uk

Bar Student Application Service (for BPTC): www.barsas.com

Bar Course Aptitude Test (BCAT): www.barstandardsboard.org.uk/qualifying-as-a-barrister/current-requirements/bar-professional-training-course/bar-course-aptitude-test

Pupillage Gateway: www.pupillagegateway.com

Funding training

Sponsorship: TARGET jobs: https://targetjobs.co.uk/career-sectors/law-solicitors/advice/305519-which-law-firms-will-fund-your-lpc-and-gdl-course-fees-and-pay-maintenance-costs

Diversity access scheme: www.lawsociety.org.uk/law-careers/diversity-access-scheme

Career development loans: www.gov.uk/career-development-loans/overview

Postgraduate loans: www.gov.uk/postgraduate-loan

Careers

www.lawcareers.net
www.simplylawjobs.com

Law reports

www.bailii.org

Useful books

University entrance

Getting into Oxford & Cambridge 2019 Entry, Trotman Education, 2018.

HEAP 2019: University Degree Course Offers, Brian Heap, Trotman Education, 2018.

How to Complete Your UCAS Application 2019 Entry, Beryl Dixon, Trotman Education, 2018.

How to Write a Winning Personal Statement, Ian Stannard, Trotman Education, 2016.

The Times Good University Guide 2018, Times Books, 2017.

The University Choice Journal, Barbara Bassot, Trotman Education, 2017.

University Interviews, Ian Stannard and Godfrey Cooper, Trotman Education, 2017.

LNAT

Passing the LNAT, R Hutton and G Hutton, Learning Matters, 2011.

Studying law

Glanville Williams: Learning the Law, A T H Smith, Sweet & Maxwell, 2010.
(This book, first published in 1945, is a very popular introductory book containing lots of useful information on studying law.)

Learning Legal Rules: A Students' Guide to Legal Method and Reasoning, 8th edition, J A Holland and J S Webb, OUP, 2013.

Letters to a Law Student: A Guide to Studying Law at University, Nicholas J McBride, Pearson, 2013.

What about Law? Studying Law at University, 2nd edition, C Barnard, J O'Sullivan and G J Virgo, Hart Publishing, 2011.

The English legal system

The Discipline of Law, Lord Denning, OUP, 2005.

The English Legal System, Jacqueline Martin, Hodder Education, 2013.

The Law Machine, Marcel Berlins and Clare Dyer, Penguin, 2000.

The Law (Theory and Practice in British Politics), J Waldron, Routledge, 1990.

Legal Method, Palgrave Macmillan Law Masters, 2013.

Politics of the Judiciary, J A G Griffith, Fontana, 2010.

The criminal justice system and miscarriages of justice

Blind Justice: Miscarriages of Justice in Twentieth Century Britain, John Eddleston, ABC-CLIO, 2000.

The Juryman's Tale, T Grove, Bloomsbury, 2000.

The Magistrate's Tale, T Grove, Bloomsbury, 2003.

A Matter of Justice, M Zander, OUP, 1989.

Memoirs of a Radical Lawyer, Michael Mansfield, Bloomsbury, 2010.

Miscarriages of Justice: A Review of 'Justice in Error', C Walker and K Starmer (eds), OUP, 1999.

Standing Accused, M McConville et al, OUP, 1994.

Careers

Is Law for You?: Deciding If You Want to Study Law, Christopher Stoakes, Christopher Stoakes Ltd, 2013.

Tomorrow's Lawyers: An Introduction To Your Future, Richard Susskind, OUP, 2013.

Professional journals

The Law Society Gazette
www.lawgazette.co.uk
(Publication for solicitors in England and Wales.)

The Lawyer
www.thelawyer.com
(A website for the legal professions containing news, analysis and comment.)

Legal Action
www.lag.org.uk/magazine
(Monthly magazine of the Legal Action Group, the access to justice charity.)

Legal Business
www.legalbusiness.co.uk
(Monthly magazine for legal professionals.)

Glossary

Administrative law
Law governing the duties and operations of the government and public authorities. A branch of public law, usually studied with constitutional law. One of the core subjects.

Advocate
A person who represents someone in court, arguing the case on their behalf. Barristers are the traditional advocates in the English legal system, but solicitors can also now conduct advocacy in certain cases. Advocates in Scotland are the equivalent of English barristers.

Bar
Collective term for the barristers' profession. Aspiring barristers are 'called to the Bar'. The Bar Council is the representative body for barristers.

Bar Professional Training Course (BPTC)
Vocational training course (of one year if studied full-time) for future barristers, taken after completing a law degree (or non-law degree followed by the Graduate Diploma in Law).

Black Letter laws
Well-established laws that are no longer in dispute.

Brexit
The prospective withdrawal of the UK from the European Union.

Chambers
Offices occupied by a group of barristers. The term also describes a group of barristers practising from a set of chambers.

Civil law
Can mean either:
- private law, as opposed to criminal, administrative, military and church law; or
- the system of law that grew from Roman law as opposed to the English system of common law.

Common law
Law derived from case law: that is, law created by judges and developed on a case by case basis, rather than laws enacted by Parliament.

Constitutional law
The rules and practices determining how the state is governed, defining the functions of the different entities within a state – i.e. the executive

(government), the legislature (Parliament) and the judiciary, and regulating the relationship between the individual and the state. The constitution of the UK remains largely unwritten, unlike most other states. It is usually studied with administrative law and is one of the core subjects.

Contract law (law of contract)
The law governing contracts, i.e. legally binding agreements (written, verbal or even implied) between two or more parties. Contracts arise as a result of offer and acceptance, although there are several other criteria that must be satisfied for an agreement to be legally binding. One of the core subjects.

Core subjects
The foundation subjects that must be studied during a degree if the degree is a Qualifying Law Degree, which satisfies the academic stage of training requirements to qualify as a lawyer. Currently these are constitutional and administrative law; contract law; tort; criminal law; equity and trusts; European Union law and property/land law.

Criminal law
The law defining those acts that are deemed to be public wrongs and are therefore punishable by the state in criminal proceedings. Most crimes are made up of two elements – the act itself (*actus reus*) and the thinking behind it (*mens rea*), both of which must be proved 'beyond reasonable doubt' in court to establish guilt. Criminal law is one of the core subjects.

Crown Prosecution Service (CPS)
The CPS, headed by the Director of Public Prosecutions (DPP), is responsible for virtually all the criminal proceedings brought by the police in England and Wales.

Delict (law of delict)
The Scottish name for tort.

Equity
The part of English law originally developed by the Lord Chancellor (and later by the Court of Chancery) to do justice where the common law remedies were limited in scope and flexibility and would lead to an unfair result: equity was more concerned with a fair result than the rigid principles of the law. Even now, equity prevails over the rules of law, but the system of equity is no longer as arbitrary as before. The main areas of equity now cover trusts, property and remedies (e.g. injunctions). 'Anton Piller' orders are a more recent example of equity at work. Equity is studied with trusts as one of the core subjects.

European Union law
The laws of the European Union and how they impact on the English legal system. One of the core subjects.

Evidence
Something that proves the existence or non-existence of a fact. The law of evidence refers to the rules governing the presentation of facts and proof in court, including whether or not evidence is admissible.

Graduate Diploma in Law (GDL)
Also known as the Common Professional Examination (CPE). The one-year (full-time) course that non-law graduates must take to satisfy the academic stage of training to become a lawyer. It covers the seven core subjects that would be studied in a qualifying law degree.

Jurisprudence
The philosophy and theories of law.

Land law (property law)
The law of rights in different types of property and how these rights may be established or transferred. It covers subjects such as mortgages, property trusts, landlord and tenant, leases, easements and covenants. One of the core subjects.

Law school
A law department within a university.

Lay jury
Group of (usually twelve) non-legally qualified people who are selected at random to give a verdict in court.

Legal Practice Course (LPC)
The vocational one-year (full-time) training course taken after graduation with a qualifying degree, or after taking the GDL, and prior to the two-year training contract, designed for intending solicitors.

Moot
A mock courtroom trial of a hypothetical case organised as an extra-curricular/optional activity to help develop legal skills of presenting a clear, logical argument and questioning a witness.

Obligations (law of obligations)
Another name for the laws of tort and contract.

Private law
The parts of the law that deal with the relationships between individuals that are of no direct concern to the state. It includes property law, trusts, contract, tort and family law.

Property law
See land law.

Public law
Law dealing with the constitution and functions of the organs of government, the relationship between individuals and the state and the relationships between individuals that are of direct concern to the state. It includes constitutional law, administrative law, tax law and criminal law.

Pupillage
The final stage of training to become a barrister, involving shadowing a qualified barrister for two six-month periods.

Statute
A law passed by Parliament.

Statute book
All statutes that are currently in force.

Tort
A wrongful act or omission for which the person who has been wronged can obtain damages (i.e. compensation) in a civil court. The definition does not include breaches of contract. Most torts involve personal injury or damage to property caused by negligence. Other torts are defamation, nuisance, etc. The law of tort is one of the core subjects.

Training contract
The two-year period of on-the-job training undertaken by all future solicitors after the LPC in order to complete the vocational stage of training.

Trusts
A legal arrangement whereby one or more trustees hold property for the benefit of one or more beneficiaries. The property is said to be held 'on trust'. Studied with equity as one of the core subjects.